JUSTIN MINOTT

with Trevor Lund

UNLEASHED

How to live fully and

do something that matters

Cover art by Christopher Evans: @goodtripinc

Dedicated to my children,
by birth and by appropriation.
May you all go further than I.

CONTENTS

PROLOGUE

In writing this book I am making a big assumption, which I hold to be true. The assumption is this: you, the reader, are enough.

You already have within you everything you need to live *Unleashed*. It lies within you in the same manner as a full tree exists within a dormant seed. You are limitless potential, which needs only the scent of water to begin bringing forth fruit. True, that part of your journey will require the darkness beneath the surface of the ground before you're ready to breach the crust of the earth, but this is a mere formality on your way to becoming a full-grown tree, providing shade to the people around you, lasting fruit to the world, and security for all those who dwell in your presence.

> *"In every block of marble I see a statue… I have only to hew away the rough walls that imprison the lovely apparition to reveal it…"* ~ Michelangelo

Your task is to engage wholly in the life-long process of unearthing what God has deposited inside of you from before you were born. All learning serves to induce the emergence of your inner greatness and to give you the tools and resources to live to your full potential.

You will thrive, not merely survive in this life, even if you happen to be a single rose blooming in the middle of an arid desert. You will bloom and it will be glorious.

The current paradigm of "education" is broken. The Latin root of education is *educo*, which implies "educe" – to evoke. Most modern education presumes a completely different foundation: precisely, that there is a teacher with a wealth of knowledge and that the role of a student is to be a sponge, an empty vessel waiting to receive information. This is not the truth. In the true sense of the word "education," teachers are meant merely to be facilitators: guides seeking to develop the latent gifts within the student, to fan the flames of the greatness already contained within the pupil. With this understanding, instead of regurgitating knowledge for you to absorb, the true hope of this volume is to stir at the hidden knowledge of your spirit and awaken the sleeping giant within. Your soul already knows what you must do.

In the same manner that Michelangelo sculpted, I write assuming that there is, and has always been, a king or a queen within you, full of limitless potential. I seek, with my words, to help chisel away at anything that is not your true self in order for you to reveal your greatness to the world. Ultimately, living *Unleashed* requires submission to the steady hand of the Great Sculptor, the One who knows exactly who you, His masterpiece, are meant to be.

By engaging the principles in this book, we will water seeds of greatness and remove limitations that stand in the way of your destiny – habits, beliefs, and destructive patterns – the weeds that seek to choke out your vastness and stand in opposition of your development. The world needs what you have.

You are enough. For this reason, I hold you capable and responsible. You are the captain of your life, under the guidance and direction of God. The Divine dwells within you. And you are enough.

Now for some housekeeping: Your reading journey through this book will begin with some of the major learning's from my life-story to provide further context and work towards the practical steps you can take to live *Unleashed*. All along the way, I'll share what I've learned from the many mentors and friends who have crossed my path. This book contains many lessons I have learned the hard way. I have already done a lot of what you should not do, hopefully so that you can avoid making the same mistakes. Some things you need to learn on your own, but experience is a brutally overrated teacher, whose lessons we often learn after it's too late. Learn from the wisdom of others, from those who have gone before you. Learn from the wisdom of your soul. I ask that you would boldly journey forward in life and make your own mistakes; do not repeat mine. And may your wonderful mistakes always be new ones rather than repetitions of your own broken patterns.

Feel free to write in this book when something speaks to you or if you don't understand something. Also, please make notes in the reflection portion at the end of each chapter. I would suggest going through this book with a friend or with a group so that you have access to different perspectives, a listening ear, and some accountability as you journey forward towards living fully and doing things that matter.

If you have questions for me, or if something resonates with you, I would love for you to let me know. This is a living document, so I invite you to add to the content by posting quotes or your own revelations to Instagram or Twitter using the hashtag **#theunleashedjourney**

Be sure to follow and tag me **@justinminott** so that I can learn from your journey, too.

It is a measurable fact that there aren't enough picture-books available for grownups. So I included cool artwork from a few of my talented friends in every chapter for you to enjoy. Follow their journey at the Instagram handle found on each image.

You'll find extra resources including a study guide at: www.justinminott.com

Let's begin.

CHAPTER 1

How to Thrive in a Cocoon

My parents were both fourteen years old when they had me. Before we get to that story, let's talk about butterflies.

The full metamorphosis of a butterfly is an incredible journey: from a mere thought in its parents' minds to life as a dependent larva, to an adolescent existence as a young caterpillar, through the darkness of a self-inflicted cocoon, into the intense struggle to be free, finally soaring into brilliant color as it learns to use its wings. Small children with nets and scientists alike have conducted studies on these fascinating creatures. Of all of these investigations, there is one scientific experiment that is particularly noteworthy as we navigate the rest of the pages in this book together.

The experiment goes as follows: two separate groups of butterflies in the final stages of their cocoon experience pass through two completely different processes – with remarkable results.

In the first group, the researchers simply and delicately open the cocoons, at the end of their development stage, on behalf of these butterflies. Note that these insects are fully mature at this point. They have reached the bittersweet end of their essential time in the isolation of the cocoon and have developed all of the biological faculties for a successful sojourn thereafter. Now we observe…

Their cocoons have been opened for them. Visualize a tired and messy bunch of developed butterflies, limping their way into their futures. Much as expected, after a short amount of time, these butterflies, which have been manually liberated from their individual dungeons, begin to exercise their wings and take flight. Around the room, they flutter and glide with elegance, as butterflies do, but this exhilaration lasts only briefly for some reason. It is not long before each and every one of our winged friends in this first observation group crashes to the cold floor, unable to regain the strength to fly again. As you can easily imagine, the life of a butter*fly* without the ability to *fly* is not sustainable; all they can ever possibly aspire to become is *butter*. So here on the floor, the fellowship is broken, and without the ability to procure sustenance, these butterflies are no more.

Now for the second group. Here the researchers took the role of the passive observer. With their scientific lab coats on and their notepads ready, they watched as this cohort began to emerge from their shells without any external help. These butterflies, fully mature like the first group, had to scratch, bite, and maneuver their way out of their dank, confined spaces. It was painstakingly slow for the scientists to watch, and terribly exhausting for the butterflies to endure. The fatigued butterflies from the first experiment looked like strapping young bucks in comparison to the sorry bunch in the second trial. Finally surfacing to the outside world from within the cocoon is highly traumatic, and it showed.

These butterflies had much more trouble getting started. The cocoon experience beat them up, left them scarred, and delayed their launch noticeably. When they did finally take flight, it was not a pretty sight. They flew a bit crooked. They fell to the ground often. But they always got back up. This group of butterflies ended up living full butterfly lives. They had the strength necessary to become airborne and to stay up there. Remember that thought.

My parents were both fourteen years old when they had me. Yes, you read correctly: 14. For any junior high students who may be reading this book – that is, if young people nowadays still read things – please know that all of the machinery works at your age. Don't play around with that stuff. In order to protect me, my biological mother, Elaine, didn't let anyone know that she was pregnant until I had been in the oven for six months.

Truthfully, Elaine didn't know *for sure* that was pregnant for a long while anyway. She had some suspicions, of course. A small protruding stomach she chalked up to the naturally occurring changes going on in her body with puberty. Her missed periods she assumed were normal because up to that point she had only ever experienced one menstrual cycle in her entire life before getting knocked up. It's cool and very weird to think that I was only her second official egg. The strange nausea that came to visit her almost every morning could have been some food aversions. But these items all put together became the clues to help solve the mystery. There are only so many times you can reasonably attribute your sickness, in the morning, to

4

some bad salmon you ate the night before. Back in those days, sex education did not begin for students that young, but at some point, you could use your logical reasoning to make an educated guess.

The news that Elaine was carrying a life inside her belly, now medically confirmed by a doctor's visit around the six-month mark of her pregnancy, triggered a series of events that shaped my destiny forever. Elaine's mom, who was with her at the doctor's office, quickly developed a very different plan for my life. Having a barely-teenager pregnant while under her jurisdiction was appalling to her. She wanted nothing to do with the social disgrace of having a grandchild conceived in the summer of 8th grade, born out of wedlock, and who would go on to have a black male as his or her father. These were some big no-nos, especially because this Canadian woman, of Anglo-Saxon heritage, was seemingly quite concerned with keeping the public illusion of togetherness in the family.

Appearance was everything for Elaine's mother. As such, she carried a palpable disdain for anything that could tarnish the family's image. It's not difficult to imagine that a bastard baby born to her fourteen-year-old daughter and a Jamaican teenager of the same age would easily earn her disapproval. Though her marriage and family life were rocky due to her husband's serious battles with addiction, she still fought tooth-and-nail to keep the façade of a strong, independent, financially stable, unshakable career woman as her primary identity. Her tumultuous circumstances left her feigning desperately for the feeling of control.

As you can imagine, to her this baby was not a blessing. This baby was an inconvenience, to put it nicely. For Elaine's mom, the decision maker in the relationship because Elaine was still a minor (by a long shot), the logical next step given the situation was for Elaine to have an abortion, to get rid of the problem altogether and go back to living a "normal" life in suburban Edmonton.

Fortunately for you and I (and unfortunately for Elaine's mom), she came up completely empty upon their visit to the first abortion specialist. He wouldn't do it. He couldn't do it. The baby was already six months along in its developmental journey in the womb. When one door closes, another one opens. So she tried taking her business elsewhere, looking to some clinics in the United States which were a little more apt to loosen their guidelines. The neighbors south of the 49th parallel have developed a bit of a reputation for pushing the boundaries further than most, sometimes towards destructive ends. She was disappointed here, too. Even our interesting neighbors to the south wouldn't kill a fetus as wonderfully developed as this one. The baby was already over two-thirds of the way along.

Ok, on to Plan B.

If they couldn't kill me, they would just get rid of me. If Elaine were to have this child, it would be a covert operation with a clean exit strategy. Elaine was transferred out of her junior high school to a pregnancy center for young teens. No one would know that I existed except for the principal of Elaine's school and one aunt (whom I would later meet). I was their best-kept secret.

With this plan, however, there was one major hurdle to overcome. Upon finding out through the school principal that his son would be a father, my biological grandfather said that he would take the child in, no questions asked. If the child belonged to his son, he would raise him or her.

Well, that wouldn't work. How could they truly get rid of this problem if he lived with his grandfather, down the street from his mother? The mother would undoubtedly be distracted from her school work by trying to visit and awkwardly semi-raise this little human who was only three months away from making his appearance in the world. No, that wouldn't work at all. So they'd have to change the story. They'd say that the father was unknown, even though there was only one young man it really could have been. They'd say there was an "incident at a party" and there was no way of knowing who the actual father was.

When I was officially placed in the system through a closed-adoption, meaning there would be no possible contact with my biological parents until I was at least 18 years old, the "unknown-father, incident-at-a-party story" was precisely the false information to be documented on my official records. My mom's mom had dodged a bullet, at least for a while.

I was born on the 22nd of March in the Misericordia hospital in Edmonton, Alberta, Canada, and was left there, hopefully for pick-up at a later date by people who would be able to give me a better opportunity at a stable life. My arrival happened to be just after a major tornado had torn through my city of birth. For most of my young life, like this tornado, I, too, swirled around destructively trying to find my way to inner peace and rest. Maybe tornados don't enjoy causing destruction. It might be that they have too much undirected, pent-up anger and energy, and they would really rather just be at rest where they can't hurt anyone or be hurt, anymore.

Thirteen days after I was born, a young couple came to take me home. They cancelled their trip to Hawaii because after years of waiting their number was finally called and they were not about to miss this opportunity. My mom, Noreen, and her husband, Ernie, had been trying to have children for the few years leading up to my adoption. The devastating result was three miscarriages and hope deferred. It's true that hope deferred makes the heart sick, as I would find out first-hand many years later when my wife and I endured a miscarriage of our own. This is a different kind of sadness because it involves mourning what would have been instead of mourning what already was. It's the beautiful anticipation of joy, the expectation of fulfillment, the future milestones, all shattered by the harsh reality of the present moment.

Now for one of my furthest reaching past memories. Here's the scene: I'm two years old and I'm curled up on my mother's lap. We are sitting together on a lightly frayed, tan colored rocking chair by a small wood-burning fireplace in the den of our bungalow. It's a quiet evening here in the "booming metropolis" of Beaumont, Alberta – a quaint town with a population of around 5,000 people at the time.

"You don't belong here," my mom gently communicates. This isn't a direct quote whatsoever, nor is it remotely close to the message she intended to communicate to my heart, but that's how it felt to grow up this way. What she actually said at this moment was more accurately, "I want you to know that your Dad and I love you very much. God brought you into our family so that we could take care of you. Your parents did what they thought was best for you, and we adopted you. We want you, and you're very special to us…" or something to that effect. All beautiful stuff. It's one thing to try and grasp these types of concept with the mind, but my heart definitely didn't understand it that way.

My mom, Noreen, is a tiny and determined woman with large, stylish, dark-rimmed glasses and medium-length light brown hair that frames her warm smile. At the absolute peak of her vertical journey, she may have only slightly surpassed the 5 foot 2-inch mark, but it would be quite foolish to judge this tiny book by its cover. Dynamite comes in small packages. She is one who loves deeply. Sometimes she hides her huge, tender heart behind a veil of firmness, but she can never keep her soft side a hidden treasure for long.

The new information about my origin was confusing. What had she meant, that my parents gave me up? Why would anyone do that? Having been a citizen of the earth for a short time at this point, I did not have much of a context for news like this. How could anyone else *also* be my mom? All of these questions were swirling around in my head, but I said little. The questions stayed deep indoors, at least for the time being.

By the time I was about five years old, God and I were tight.[1] I had no grand concept of religion, really, or on theories of social organization. All I know is that God was so real to me, not because anyone else had convinced me so, but because I hung out with Him every day. Singing and talking with Him from the comfort of my bed into the late hours of the night (sometimes until after 9 p.m.!), I could sense Him right there with me. It's hard to describe a closeness like

---

[1] Note that for simplicity throughout the book I refer to the Divine Presence mostly using the word God, and through the use of the pronouns He and Him. I acknowledge that language is incomplete in describing someone/something who exists beyond words. In your reading, please substitute for whatever allows you to digest the material of the book. Call Him/Her/It by what is helpful for you: be it God, Allah, Life Force, Higher Power, Ultimate Reality, etc. – or disregard it altogether if that's more helpful.

He and I shared, but the feeling of secure bliss that accompanied being with Him was like nothing else in the world.

As I got older, my personal path into the heart of the Divine led through the person of Jesus. I heard about Jesus in a small church that we attended as a family in our hometown. The fact that God would come to earth and take on human form to die for everyone, past, present, and future, just so that we could be free to be in close relationship with the Creator was breathtaking. I was taught that because God is perfect, and we're not even close to perfect, the way to get back into a healthy relationship with God is through what His Son, Jesus, accomplished by dying on the cross and rising from the dead. With Him we're able to break free from our destructive patterns and live fully.

He took on all of my mess so that I could be with Him and join Him in His amazing, redemptive mission of reconciling people to God, to their true selves. It was beautiful. I found this story to be awesome and of the utmost importance, so I decided to prayerfully give my life to Jesus at least once a week, reminding Him that I was really serious, whenever I remembered to. This went on until my skateboard-loving elementary school friend, Nick, told me that technically, according to most theology, I only had to give my life to Him once by saying a special prayer.

Ok, fine. I just wanted to be sure that He knew I was all in. And even now to this day, the more I walk with Him, the more I realize that we have to choose Him and His way daily, in the smallest of moments. It's a path to walk. It's a way of being. It really isn't a one-time decision or some fancy prayer that we have to pray. All of those serve as tools and can be helpful steps along the journey. Abundant life is found in the little decisions to follow His leading. We have a choice to reject or honor our Creator in the tiniest of actions (or inactions) every day. I'm not sure that there is some sort of "in" versus "out" for people based on saying some magic words. Following Him is a way of life.

Fast-forward some more. I was seven years old and I started to notice a few more things. My hair was much curlier than that of my brother and sister, named Jarrett and Jinessa respectively. Now is actually a great time to get you acquainted with these two wonderful humans.

Jarrett has a raspy voice. He's undersized due to the fact that he was born four and a half months early. But he's always been an eager fella who knows no limitations. Born legally blind and with Cerebral Palsy, he wears thick glasses, which have what seems to be the magnifying power of a telescope, and he is developmentally delayed for his age, whatever that means. He is simply incredible and consistently defies all odds. He went from not being expected to walk, talk, or even survive, to somehow safely-ish riding his bike to high school, playing basketball, and holding a meaningful job at the local grocery store. His life and accomplishments continue to push boundaries.

My dear sister, Jinessa, the youngest of the bunch and the princess of our home, is an absolute bundle of joy. The way she pronounced her words as a kid almost made it sound like she had a British accent. She keeps the order in our three-kid gang by telling Mom on me when she feels I have broken the law of the land and by reminding me of the rules often. Somehow this little girl with strawberry blonde hair has superhuman stamina: she is able to watch the same movie more times in a row than anyone I have ever met, her favorite choice of the era being a classic film starring Mary-Kate and Ashley Olsen called *It Takes Two*.[2] Jinessa is one of the most kind-hearted humans I've ever met with a strong passion for social justice. I'm so proud of who she is.

Yes, so I noticed that my hair was much curlier than theirs was and I resolved that in order to fit in, I should get a buzz-cut to get rid of as much as possible. The problem with hair as curly as mine was that even when the barber cut it low, the hair still formed little waves on the top of my head. So I did everything in my power to make my hair 'normal'. I tried putting hair-gel in it and combing it down. That didn't work. I cut it lower the next time. That didn't work. No matter what I did, I just couldn't make myself look like everyone else in my family.

Think about what it's like to look in the mirror and have no idea what you're really looking at. I might have my mother's nose. I could have my dad's bushy eyebrows. But I had no clue where any of this came from. I felt like Frankenstein's monster: a creature of sorts with no apparent ties to the natural world and with no real context within which to exist. As far as I was concerned, I had no origin. How was I supposed to know where I was going if I didn't know where I was coming from? I consider my brother and sister to be blood-family to me, both were born naturally to Noreen and Ernie after I was adopted. They are still my people and will be forever. Yet there remained a huge piece of me that felt out of place even within my own family. Really, it's that I felt out of place in this world altogether.

---

[2] We recently watched this movie as a family at our Thanksgiving celebration and she still remembers almost every line in the movie.

@tai.the.girl

ouch.

Then things start getting rough with our Dad. I didn't notice it as much before this, but the way he is acting is not right at all. His name is Ernie. He is a broad-shouldered, stocky man with weathered skin and jet-black hair, which contained naturally occurring grey 'highlights'. When he is good, he is good. But when he is off, he is way off. He bought me my first fishing rod for my fifth birthday and to this day I still have a deep love for fishing. The problem was the dichotomy. Ernie is either throwing a ball with me, or he is throwing punches at me.

The abuse gets progressively worse, verbal and physical. Most of the abuse is directed at my mom. I get all of the second-hand smoke. The leftover abuse is primarily directed at me, because I'm the oldest and I speak up about issues.

As I write, I realize that I've had to fight hard to recover the gift of speaking my mind over the years. I have a propensity to defend the defenseless and fighting inequity. I guess it is actually possible to beat something out of someone with enough persistence (like confidence, or self-love, or my propensity for speaking up), or at least to send it down to the depths where it can only come back through a process of healing, forgiveness, and digging for the suppressed and hidden gold of the soul. It was precisely my strong sense of *justice*, which is the meaning of my name, after all, that led to Ernie's wrath as I tried to protect my Mom and my siblings.

I found a way to navigate the duplicity of my private/public life by the time I had reached the fourth grade. My old report cards from the earlier grades reflect an aptitude for learning, but I can easily cross-reference what was going on in our home situation by the comments I received in those reports. When I started receiving comments on my report cards to the effect of, "Justin is helpful and smart, but he gets distracted easily and sometimes acts out," it just so happens that that is precisely when life started getting rough with Ernie. To the teachers out there, or really to anyone working with (or raising) young people, please keep in mind that when a flower isn't blooming we shouldn't blame the flower. Look deeper into its environment and conditions. I'm convinced that kids don't set out wanting to be "bad."

By the fourth-grade, one of my teachers thought that I was such a gifted student that I should skip the fifth-grade. This was a beautiful idea in principle. I would get to graduate early. I would be challenged at a higher level. Know that I have no regrets about my life, but this plan backfired a bit. It's great to be a bit uncomfortable; that's how we grow. But there is something to be said about the confidence a child receives from being at or near the top of his class, of being a shark in a fishpond. I went straight from that amazing feeling to the feeling of being a baby bird drowning in a shark tank. I was completely out of place and out of my league. It wasn't because there were suddenly many students above me academically, I could still hold my own in the learning department; it was because I entered an environment that made me seriously doubt if it was even worth being smart anymore. With these new classmates, smart wasn't cool.

I was ten years old when the police found Ernie's truck by a bridge with no trace of him anywhere. Leading up to this moment, Noreen finally had to get a restraining order issued against him because our lives were in constant danger. My mom is a principled woman who fully believed in, and lived, the notion of "till death do us part." He had threatened to light our house on fire (among other threats), so she finally had to make the tough decision to protect her children above all else.

It was the fifth grade for me at this time. We were pulled out of school because the police hadn't found his body and we didn't know if he was still alive, plotting some sort of sinister plan against our family. So we had to hide in plain sight, right in a nearby city. I told my friends we were going on a family vacation. No one knew what was going on at home, not even my closest friends. Even still many of them would be surprised to learn this story. We were masters of deception for the purpose of self-preservation and keeping a decent family image in our community. My mom, my two siblings, and I checked into the Ramada hotel in Edmonton for a week. Every time we saw a dark Ford truck drive by we thought it was him. It was an awful week on the nerves to be sure.

Ernie was a tormented soul suffering from a serious mental illness, most likely a personality disorder. Sometimes he was a loving father, like when he got me that fishing rod for my fifth birthday so that we could spend quality time fishing together. Other times, I would have to go to school wearing a turtleneck sweater and dark glasses to cover up the bruises. We never knew which Ernie we were going to get at any given moment, which, as you can imagine, is extremely emotionally taxing. We spent a lot of emotional energy looking for clues as to who our dad was every minute, and we tried to adjust our behavior accordingly.

I couldn't manage to cry at his funeral. Something had snapped inside of me. So immediately upon his death, and without anyone else's prompting, I unhealthily gave myself the title and role of "man of the house." I wanted to be strong for my mom and siblings, so I wrestled with my conflicting emotions as stoically as I could muster the strength for at the time. It's a weird feeling, that of being oddly relieved that someone found your father's corpse, that Dad was now gone forever. I guess I was relieved because the struggle was over, for us and for him. I was fatherless, again, but I was safe. It's just unfortunate that those two realities were mutually exclusive for me.

I was also angry. I was mad at God for the cards I had been dealt. I was mad at the world for being a terrible place. I was mad at myself, thinking that I must have been the cause of so much destruction and pain. It seemed that everywhere I was there happened to be an abundance of issues and loss in the near vicinity. At some point, a young man in such circumstances can easily believe he's the real problem.

I started drinking hard alcohol in my bedroom at the age of 11. It tasted awful but it took the edge off, if only temporarily. I started smoking marijuana shortly thereafter. I sat in my room listening to only the angry Tupac lyrics. He seemed to be the only person who understood me at all. I did anything I could do to numb the constant, searing pain caused by my deep, unhealed emotional wounds. When most well-meaning people approach the subject of addictions, they usually ask, "Why the addiction?" That's the wrong question. The correct question is, "Why the pain?"

When I was about 12 years old, my mother, Noreen, met a "terrible" man named Keith. I say he was "terrible," because he is actually quite lovely and it was annoying at the time. He's an incredible man who loves our family with his whole heart, who fathered us as well as he possibly could, who introduced me to the beauty of music, who rode his motorcycle 9 hours in the rain just to see one of my playoff football games in another province. He's incredible.

But that's not the point. At the time, from my perspective, he was terrible. Here comes this intruder, this foreign substance invading the comfort and predictability of our unstable home. I certainly wasn't as welcoming then as I am now. For me as a teenage boy, who had unhealthily taken up the mantle of "man of the house," this dude was on my turf and I didn't like that one bit. For example, once when Keith told me not to be disrespectful towards my Mom, I told him something along the lines of: "Don't come in here thinking you own the place. I'm still the man of the house…" and so on… Teenagers. Mom and Keith got married shortly thereafter and I've grown to love him deeply over the years as we've walked through life together. (Don't tell him that.)

The next few years were some of the worst. I had developed the skill of appearing like I was OK, and I was getting better at it every day. Inside I was tormented and alone. On the outside, I was making jokes and helping everyone else through their problems. I got in a lot of trouble at home and at school, not the big kind of trouble, but enough to make people pay attention to me. If only they had known that I was in so much pain.

As a teenager, dealing with feelings of rejection and abandonment wasn't easy. I didn't let anyone get close enough to me to know what was really going on because then any future rejection or abandonment would hurt less. They couldn't hurt me if I kept them at a good enough distance from my heart, right? But in the depths of my being, I longed to be known and appreciated for who I really was. This was a paradox because I simultaneously didn't trust anyone. I wanted to be known, but I effectively and unconsciously sabotaged anything that would let people past the massive walls I'd built. Much like the human body rejects viruses without mental forethought, the heart rejects anything it views as a threat to its well-being – even when the heart is wrong about what it classifies an impending danger.

I lived with a chip on my shoulder, using Tupac's album title *Me Against the World* as my undeclared motto. As far as I was concerned, it *was* me (and God, when I wasn't mad at Him) against everyone else. No one could be trusted. The scary thing was that I became amazing at letting people into my life *just enough* so they genuinely thought they knew me. I was incredible at faking vulnerability. It was the best way to keep them off of my scent. And they were none the wiser.

I was drinking, doing drugs, selling drugs, acting out in school, trying to be popular, doing anything to fill the void I had in my heart. I did barely enough work to keep decent grades in school. Thankfully I have a sharp mind so I could get average grades with less effort. I wasn't necessarily suicidal at any point, but I lived recklessly as though it wouldn't matter if I walked out in front of a car. I didn't care about life. I didn't love myself. How could someone make healthy decisions and choose good paths in life when he doesn't see his existence as valuable? It's near impossible. If you don't value something, you don't take care of it. That's human nature. I didn't think I was worth valuing at all. Why would I be? My own parents gave me up. So I gave up on myself.

Thank God for football. I was lucky enough to have the great O.J. Lepps as my high school coach. He's a one-eyed black man who has overcome countless obstacles to achieve what he has in life and a man who is truly a maker of men and not just a coach to high school football players. The football field was my sanctuary. There, with the smell of fresh cut grass beneath my feet, with the rush of action, I was free. I would hit people with all of the anger that I had inside of me.

It was at the end of my rookie season that Coach Lepps approached me and spoke words that helped change the trajectory of my life forever: "Justin, you're a leader. Put in the work over the offseason because I believe you can be a captain on this football team." That was it. He saw something in me that I didn't know was there. He saw beyond the scrawny, angry, young man that stood before him, and saw a warrior. I trained harder that summer than I ever knew was possible because I now had some vision for my life, at least in this one area. When I returned in the fall, I was equipped with a ton of muscle and hustle. I became a leader.

Still, success off of the football field was elusive. I hated schoolwork. I was failing English and staying just below average in the rest of my classes.[3] My parents and I could never see eye to eye. I had this lingering belief in the back of my mind that I didn't belong anywhere, even in my own family.

Then suddenly, what I would call an encounter of the third-kind changed my life forever. I was seventeen years old when it happened. I had occasionally been attending a Christian youth group some Friday nights, often going there high on weed and pretending I didn't want to be there at all. The youth pastors, Marty and Krista, were some of the first people who took the time to love me just for who I was. Marty and I started meeting regularly and his whole agenda was love. He wasn't trying to change me but was truly invested in helping

---

[3] If you happen to be one of my high school English teachers reading this, I'm sure it's blowing your mind to know that I actually spent time *writing* on my own accord. Also, sorry and thank you. You are saints for not expelling me.

me become the best version of who God created me to be. It was refreshing. For the few years up until this point, my relationship with God was rocky at best. I was still attending a church and I was playing drums for the worship band on Sunday mornings, but more often than not I was still somewhat hung-over from the night before.

It seemed like nothing would ever change. Then everything changed in a moment. I had just finished attending a youth group event and I was feeling uncontrollably angry for the crappy cards life had dealt me. I wanted to do something stupid. I didn't know what, I just knew that I was in a destructive mood. One of my friends brought me to Marty and asked him if he would pray for us. We went for a car ride and we ended up praying in a school parking lot in my hometown.

I have no way to explain this to people who haven't had an encounter with the supernatural world, but this experience felt more real than life itself. It was as though a huge weight was being lifted off of my shoulders. My heart started feeling free, as though talons that had been gripping it tight for years now had to let go of their grip. My soul felt a peace unlike anything else I've experienced. I felt God's love. It was tangible. It was palpable. And I've never been the same since.

His audacious love is still transforming my life. I guess that's what happened to countless people who met Jesus while He walked this earth. One encounter with Him and life can never be the same. We can choose to hate Him. We can try to ignore Him. But we can't deny Him once we've experienced His wonderful presence. I was at a junction. He pursued me and chose me. What would I do in response to His relentless love? In response, I chose Him. I chose to follow Him and His way of life forever. I chose what Robert Frost calls "the road less traveled" and it has made all the difference...

Now back to the butterflies.

As humans, we mostly subscribe to the notion that when people overcome difficult obstacles and somehow manage to reach the heights of achievement, they have done so *in spite of* their unfortunate circumstances. They managed to make it through the muck and the mire with perseverance and grit, and have attained the great feats that they have even though they faced overwhelming obstacles. We know the familiar characters: Beethoven composing masterpieces as a deaf man, Barack Obama becoming the President of the United States as a fatherless minority, Helen Keller learning to speak and changing the world for so many others as a blind, deaf woman. These people beat the odds with the whole world stacked against them. What a feat! Or is it?

What if these people have reached these pinnacles of success, not *in spite of* their circumstances, but rather *because of* their circumstances?[4]

As it turns out, the second group of butterflies, the ones who had to struggle and fight just to survive, were ultimately equipped with the right tools to soar. I propose that they didn't succeed *in spite* of their pain. Instead, they succeeded precisely *because of* their pain. The path

---

[4] Malcolm Gladwell has a whole book called *David and Goliath* dedicated to the advantages of being an underdog.

of utmost resistance managed to forge in this second group a stamina that the first group of butterflies simply didn't have. The awful experience of the cocoon appeared to set them back at the beginning of their new journey, but it is precisely that experience which gave them the strength to live fully. Let's not forget that the first experimental group consisted of fully developed butterflies before they all came up short. They were endowed with seemingly all of the right stuff (read into this: connections, talents, natural abilities, resources, etc.) but they lacked one critical element to true maturity: healthy struggle. And they were far worse off for it.

This makes me thankful that I'm not a full-time astronaut. In order to stay in shape while in the zero gravity environment, astronauts have to train extra hard just to maintain their basic fitness levels. Zero gravity means there's no natural resistance. In that environment, it's easy to become weak because there are no forces acting against one's muscles to make them work at all. If you find yourself in a situation where you have little or no resistance in your life, it's probably time to find something that will challenge you to grow. It is way too easy to become complacent in zero-gravity-type situations. But let's face it, the concept of willingly exercising sounds terrible. Think about it, when we exercise, the strain we endure produces microscopic tears in our muscles. That sounds awful, except for the fact that after some rest, these tears heal back together stronger than before, producing muscular growth, enhanced capacity, and increased endurance.

We would do well to live what Theodore Roosevelt called "the strenuous life" – a life committed to pushing our limits – in order to uncover our larger potential. For me, I know that I am the man I am today because of adversity. Nothing besides the tremendous gift of suffering, both solicited and unsolicited by me, could have adequately equipped me with the strength, resilience, and perspective I now possess. Pressure is what changes coal into a diamond, turning this object of seemingly low value into a rare commodity. For humans, the right type of pressure forces us to get creative, to adapt, and to think outside the box. It forces us to grow.

In the same way that we strengthen our muscles through resistance training, God uses hardships to strengthen our soul. While I would never wish the pain of fatherlessness, abandonment, or abuse on anyone, I would not trade my life in for anyone else's. Knowing what I know today, on this side of my past, I would go through it all again if I knew that my journey would be able to help even one person who struggling through similar issues in his or her life. If you're reading this and you happen to be that one person who is getting some value out of my story, know that to me you're worth it all.

Now we get to the crux of the matter; the crossroads we all must face. We still have to choose what we to do with our stories.

My history (and even my current difficulties for that matter) as challenging as it may have been, only holds as much power over my future as I let it. A story is like a brick. A brick is neutral. By itself, it is neither good nor bad. What I do with the brick gives it its power. I can use a brick to smash a window. I can also use a brick to build a house. It can be a destructive force or it can be a constructive force. Whether the brick has a negative or positive effect lies completely in my hands.

My past hasn't changed. I have no power to change it. The only thing that changed to help me live *Unleashed* was a change in perspective on my story. It's the same story. It's the same brick. What I choose to do with it makes all of the difference. I now use my story to speak hope into the lives of thousands of people around the world through motivational speaking and workshops. In using my story to write this book, it has the potential to unleash peoples' dreams all around the world. I'm using the perseverance and fearlessness born out of my struggles to run international businesses that make a difference in the lives of thousands. I use my pain and experiences to write music that resonates with people's hearts. I refuse to let my past determine my future. In the same way, a rock can either be a stumbling block that you trip over for the rest of your life, an excuse to underachieve, or it can be a stepping-stone which you stand on, raising you to new heights. It's still the same rock. What you do with it is up to you.

PRINCIPLE #1: OWN YOUR STORY

A pastor and mentor of mine, Rev. Brian Warren, often says, "People see the glory but they don't know the story." And it's true. People see your success. People see your achievements. People see your accomplishments. Or they see and judge your shortcomings. But they have no idea the fight you had to endure just to be who you are, doing the things you are doing, where you are doing them. They have no idea how difficult it was for you to get out of bed and function like a normal person on days when you were fighting depression.

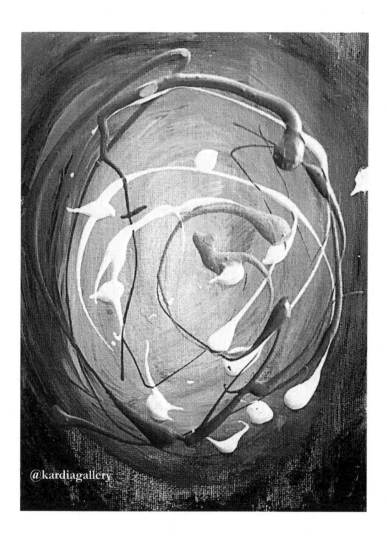

@kardiagallery

They have no idea what it took for you to focus in school when you didn't eat breakfast because there was no food in your house. They have no idea how hard it was to fit-in in a new country that you didn't even want to move to, with a brand new language, and a completely different way of life. Whatever it is, they have no idea. And that's OK.

Note that your struggle is your struggle. As humans, we love comparing ourselves to others. In reading my story, you may have had thoughts like, "Oh, well I've never gone through anything that difficult," or conversely, "That's not bad; you should hear what I've been through," and neither mindset is necessarily helpful for growth. Life is about acceptance. It's about accepting who you are and what you've been through, and assertively making choices to move forward towards your destiny. Don't discount your struggles. And don't overestimate your struggles. They are yours, and you are exactly where you are right now, and that is enough.

Your struggle is not in vain. The difficult circumstances you've faced, and are facing even now, will not be wasted. I don't say this with a shallow, 'everything happens for a reason' mindset, but I do know that God is a perfect steward who can use anything to make beauty. You will use your story to positively impact many lives. Your pain is further equipping you for the greatness that you are meant to achieve. Great adversity may be an indicator that you are destined to reach even higher elevation.

In the same way that tough circumstances can deepen the roots of a tree, the harsh situations in your life have the potential to deepen the roots of your soul. When a tree has to struggle to find water, it sends its roots even deeper. When storms come, its roots go deeper still in order to brace the tree against the elements. Then, when the tree does grow in stature, it has the necessary foundation to remain rooted. In order to grow taller, our roots must go deeper. Otherwise, the larger storms to come at the higher levels can topple us much more easily. The higher a tree grows, the more exposed to the elements it becomes, especially as it reaches out from within the safe, protective canopy of the rest of the forest. You require more depth in order to gain more height. The higher the calling, the deeper the roots must be to maintain your destiny.

Of course, there are times when an overly harsh environment can do too much damage to a person. But that's not for you. You're still here, and you're reading this book, and to me, that's enough of a sign that there's more for you than what you're currently going through. Often, your greatest struggles catapult you into your greatest areas of influence. Even a deficiency in one area can give you superpowers in another. For example, dyslexic people usually develop a greater aptitude for remembering facts by honing in their listening faculties rather than through comprehension of written material. Or high-energy people who tend to have trouble focusing, like me, develop an aptitude for performing well when crunched for time. Even our weaknesses can produce strengths.

God is in the capacity development business. He has greater feats for you to accomplish so He's equipping you with the strength you need. In the moment, it's hard to "consider it pure joy...whenever you face trials of many kinds..." (James 1:2), but it is absolutely true that these trials produce perseverance. And when perseverance has completed its work in you, you end up mature and complete, not lacking anything. Like exercise, the results of adversity are worth it.

Though it may cause pain and discomfort in the moment, you are getting stronger.

Do not shy away from your story. Do not seek to make it seem worse than it is. Do not try to make it seem better than it is.

Your story simply *is*. Own it and use it. Tell your story to help others realize that you're human and to help people find their way on their own path.

> *"...and just when the caterpillar thought the world was over, it became a butterfly."* ~ *Unknown*

REFLECTION:

What is the real story of my life's narrative, pain and all?
And how can I use my story to help others?

CHAPTER 2

How to Make Lemonade

I felt like my life was in shambles. I had just come through a disorienting and difficult year, maybe the most challenging season of my leadership journey to date. Our company, Good Coffee, was struggling terribly. Nothing was working out the way I had planned in any of my other ventures. I was dropping the ball on a bunch of my responsibilities, failing at almost every turn. I couldn't seem to balance being a good husband, human, entrepreneur, or any of my other key roles. I felt like I was at least one step behind on everything I was doing. Many of my relationships with the people I cared about were suffering. I was struggling to find direction and purpose. And my side of the bedroom was a complete disaster, which is usually a pretty good indicator of how I'm doing overall. It was absolute chaos.

As far as I was concerned, the most logical solution was to press the restart button. I had totally failed so I needed a fresh start. I wasn't necessarily entertaining suicidal thoughts, but the honest truth is that the idea of quitting life here on earth passed through my mind at least once a week. I wasn't about to actually quit life, but that path seemed appealing at times considering the alternative of doing the difficult work required to fix all of the things in my life that were broken. At the very least, I wanted to run away somewhere far away, where nobody knew who I was. I wanted to abandon everything that had anything to do with responsibility so that I would never find myself this overwhelmed again. I wanted to be in a position where no one expected anything from me so I couldn't possibly continue letting anyone down. No more trying to make a difference. Therefore no more doing anything that could hurt anyone.

I wanted to make a mad dash in the opposite direction of my problems however I could. The only problem with that approach is that problems don't ever go away by ignoring them. Running away from our problems accomplishes nothing because the true roots of our problems lie within us. No matter what, no matter where we go, if the issues are unresolved or if we haven't learned the lesson we needed to learn from a given situation, the same things will manifest right where we are. Even on an island all by ourselves, we'd find a way to create the same issues. Furthermore, by my disengaging life, I would have robbed myself of whatever assignments God has for me. It turns out there was only one way forward, and I got my clue from looking at the way God handled His own mess.

According to the Genesis account of creation, God had some serious chaos to deal with right from the very beginning:

"In the beginning, God created the heavens and the earth. Now the earth was formless and empty, and chaos covered the deep. And the Spirit of God was hovering over the deep waters. Then God said, 'Let there be light.' And there was light." ~ Genesis 1:1-4

After this, God continues to speak a series of "Let there be" statements and whatever He says goes. Everything He speaks becomes a reality. In re-reading this story, I was struck with the materials God was using in the beginning to create our beautiful world. His canvas was "formless and empty" and He was using "chaos" as His medium of choice.

Read it again. That's what it says. You would think it would make more sense for God to throw out the formless, empty, chaotic world and start from scratch, creating things out of nothing, like He did to kick-start the universe. But that's not at all what He did. He took a bleak, hopeless, messy situation and formed it into something new. He spoke order into the chaos and caused it to take breathtaking shape.

Everything we see around us in nature – magnificent sunsets, majestic mountains, the powerful rolling rivers, flowers that cause you to stop and take notice, birds, bees, animals… and even you and I – is made out of re-formed chaos. God is in the business of taking despair and giving it shape, meaning, and life.

In the moments when our life seems shapeless and void and chaos is covering every aspect, even when the chaos found in the deepest recesses of our heart, there is hope.

> *"He has made everything beautiful in its time."*
> ~ *Ecclesiastes 3:11*

The most interesting thing about the Genesis account of creation is that God never removes the chaos. Instead, He uses it and turns it into something beautiful. All it takes is one word from God, one "Let there be" statement, and everything in our life must begin to come into alignment and take shape. Instead of running from the pain and hurt we experience, we need to learn to treat it how God does: learn how to lean into situations instead of checking out and to reshape the tough moments into something beautiful.

PRINCIPLE #2: LEAN INTO THE MESS

I can testify to this truth because every time I share my story I get to repurpose some of the most difficult situations in my life to help others move forward in their lives. When life gives you lemons, you can make a lot more than lemonade. Take the seeds and plant an entire lemon grove. Some people see the challenge in every opportunity. Others see the opportunity in every challenge. Find the possibility of beauty even in the darkest and emptiest moments.

Now is the time to lean into the mess in our life and engage, with God, in rejuvenating all that is broken. Dig deep. Put one foot in front of the other and move forward. Don't be afraid of the chaos. Use it. Get creative with it. Have the courage to journey into the dark places of your life to find healing and restoration. No more avoiding life. No more running.

There comes a point when we can no longer spend our time searching for ways to skirt *around* the dark forest in our soul, and everyone has at least one dark place in there. We must go *through* the darkness in order to find deeper freedom. All of us have (mostly unconsciously) developed varying avoidance strategies depending on our personality type because we are afraid of what we will find in the depths of our hearts if we were to do some real digging. If, however, we are serious about becoming whole and living *Unleashed*, we must press into our own darkness to discover lasting light. The remedy for whatever happens to be our coping mechanism usually involves a decision to intentionally turn around and start walking in the other direction.

For those of us who cope by trying to control the world through perfectionism, we must seek the pleasure that comes from the tranquility of lettings things be and resisting the need to be perfect or right.

For those of us who need to be needed and recognized, who cannot stand being alone, we must find time for the healing power of true solitude to work its way through our souls and to serve others without expecting anything in return.

For those of us who avoid facing our demons by striving for the appearance of success through achievement, we must embrace the humility of our humanity and have the courage to show others our true selves, weaknesses and all.

For the creative ones among us who cloak our melancholy sadness with aesthetic and the overemphasized need to be perceived as unique, we must seek balance and emotional stability in order to sort out our feelings and communicate our deep, burning truths in ways which endure.

For those of us who tend to retreat into the safe, mental fortress of our thoughts through reflective seclusion in avoidance of interdependency, we must learn to lean on others and force ourselves to express our authentic feelings as best as we can muster.

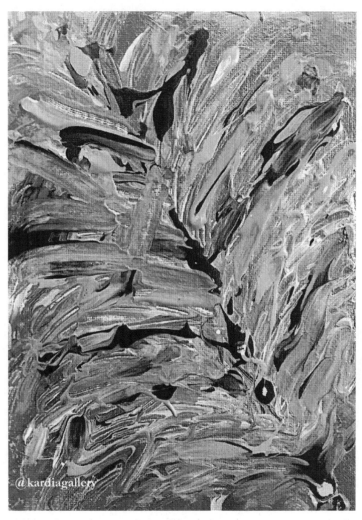

For those of us who chase the illusion of security and safety, grasping for control by building our walls higher when life gets uncomfortable, we must find the courage that comes from deeper surrender and trust in the capable One who holds our lives in His hands.

For those of us who avoid pain using uncontrolled optimism and pleasure-seeking, we must, in sobriety, turn and face the darkness in our lives to experience richer, more sincere joy on the other side.

For those of us who cope using anger, seeking to inflict pain on others in empty attempts to numb our own, we must seek to give mercy and experience the marvelous freedom of accepting others for who they are and forgiving those who have wronged us.

For those of us who turn to comfort, sleep, and distraction to avoid facing the harsh realities of life, we must be fully awake and reflective long enough to look at what is really going on beneath the calm surfaces we project to the world.

This list is not near exhaustive, but you get the picture. In general, we find growth in the opposite direction of what is comfortable to us. Our highest selves are not exaggerated versions of our current deficiencies, but rather redeemed, refined, functional, and balanced expressions of our gifts, fully *Unleashed* to serve others in healthy ways. The journey of growth takes us towards an increasingly complete and whole state of being where we experience the fullness of who we are meant to be, focused and channeled like sunlight through a magnifying glass to increase the intensity of our inner light.

Problems don't go away when we ignore them. If we engage in the painful process of pressing into our issues, though, we find even more beauty waiting for us on the other side of the issue.

Whatever the mess is, lean into it. Have that hard conversation. Face your dark past. Admit your deepest fear. Even the act of exposing the issue does a great deal to shrink it down to a manageable size. Light and truth transform a seemingly insurmountable mountain into a climbable hill.

Lean in. The most beautiful places in the world are often the most difficult to get to. So it is with the inner work of the soul.

> *"Crawl if you can't walk… just move forward."*
> *~ Martin Luther King Jr.*

REFLECTION:

What problems or pain am I avoiding right now?

How beautiful could life be on the other side of my struggle?

CHAPTER 3

How to Hate your Birthday

I knew something was terribly wrong with me. After all, who, in their right mind hates their birthday? Most kids are uncontrollably excited, figuring out which of their acquaintances deserve the honor of attending their party, along with choosing which colorful party hats and kazoos to give as favors. For me, there were many years that my friends found out about my birthday in passing, usually later on in the week after it had passed and the storm blew over. I never really knew why I felt this way. I just knew that every year at the time of my birthday, I was overwhelmed with deep apathy and resignation.

Hating your birthday is not normal. So, like a patient concerned at noticing problematic symptoms, I started digging deeper towards the cause. Why would any kid avoid celebrating, or even allowing others to celebrate, the day of their birth? After probing the recesses of my heart, it turned out that I had believed an extremely damaging story about the day I exited the womb and made my appearance into the land of the living officially.

Here's how I viewed the scene. Picture a completely dull-grey, dreary, hospital room with no interesting pictures on the wall. In the creaky bed was my birth-mom, apathetic. She gives birth to a baby boy and there is zero fanfare. No one is getting excited about this kid. "Congratulations! He's 8 pounds, 10 ounces," said no one ever. No one is giving anyone cool helium balloons and saying, "Isn't he the cutest little nugget you've ever seen?" If social media had been around at that time, no one would've clicked 'like' on the photo. In fact, the photo would have never been posted. After this remarkably unexciting entrance to the world, my mom leaves me in the hospital and goes back to her life as if nothing had happened. My conclusion: I wasn't celebrated.

Of course, none of this is true. The look of the hospital room is the only potentially accurate piece of that story only because I'm not sure how they decorated hospital rooms back then so I couldn't confirm or deny. But what's true doesn't really matter, certainly not as much as it logically should when it comes to our identities.

Our interpretation of reality is even more important than reality itself. Our construed memories and analysis of our circumstances are inexplicably powerful in shaping our identities, whether they're accurate or not. We shape our futures with the conclusions we draw from our past. The actual events only have as much power over us as we let them through our creative interpretations and inferences.

From the understanding of our circumstances, we form ideas about who we are, who God is, and our place on this planet. Information inferred from our painful memories can, if we let it, become the distorted lens through which we interpret our present situation. This pain becomes the looking-glass through which we project our future, often through a destructive cycle of continually reinforced self-fulfilling prophecies.

What do I believe about myself, or about God, or about life, based on my experiences? For me, I took a largely invented version of my birth story and conceived extremely harmful deductions about my existence. I reasoned that because, in my twisted understanding, I wasn't celebrated, I was, therefore, not worth celebrating. And this is just one of many distorted stories I adopted as truth in my life, often to my detriment.

Consider the great mountain of consequences that could stem from this seemingly harmless pebble of an idea. When you don't think you're worth celebrating, you interpret other people's actions as though they're deliberately not acknowledging your worth and inherent value. This can result either in pride that puffs up the ego and wrongly asserts itself, or a recoiling so that you don't put yourself out there and risk being forgotten or abandoned again. That became my paradigm. Looking back, I can see myself engaged in using both the pride and the self-loathing as coping mechanisms for the pain of feeling worthless, which usually led me down destructive paths. I was living with an unhealthy drive to succeed in an attempt to justify my existence by proving to the world, and to myself, that I deserve to be here. And the results were predictably disastrous. I hurt myself. I hurt others. I struggled to find peace.

I lived like this for years until one glorious day those chains were broken.

As we've seen so far, living *Unleashed* means we must first own our stories and accept our pasts. We also have to lean into the broken places in our lives instead of running from our problems. But how do we move forward in areas where there is a real pain that still holds us back?

What I'm about to relate to you is one of my most profound and shaping spiritual experiences to date.

As you can imagine, the understanding of the "why" behind my actions was really only the beginning of a scary and freeing journey into the depths of my soul. God began leading me deeper into the dark caves of my heart, wherein lay the roots of my behaviors. Soul-work gets heavier and far more fruitful once we begin to uncover the roots behind our actions

I felt prompted to mentally revisit the scene of my birth. So I sat. I closed my eyes. And I pictured the gloomy scene, the part of my story where I was left unwanted in the hospital room. I asked God a simple question. "When I was abandoned as a newborn in my most vulnerable state, where were you? ...No, seriously, where the hell were you?!" I demanded. "And why would you let this happen to me?"

As I wallowed in my deep anger, I started to sense His overwhelming love fill the room and cover me like a warm blanket. Then, ever so graciously, He showed me what was really going on in His world at that time. He showed me the truth.

He said, "My son, it may have looked to you like no one was celebrating your arrival, that there was no excitement in the room, but, man, you should have seen the party I was having. I was overjoyed! I said, 'Hey! Everyone look; my boy is finally here! We're going to have a blast changing the world together. I've been so looking forward to this moment. My son is here!' It was beautiful."

"And furthermore," He continued, "You've been focusing on this idea that you weren't wanted because they tried to get rid of you by having an abortion. Instead, I need you to understand the fact that I wanted you here so badly that I had to hide you in your mother's womb for six months just to get you here. I had to smuggle you in because I just *had* to have you here."

I wept.

He celebrated me. And I got this deep sense that it was the ugly-excited kind of celebrating, like when you're thrilled to the point that you're completely undignified and lose the sense of who's around you. Like when Tom Cruise jumped up and down on Oprah's couch. It was that kind of celebrating times infinity.

When the King of the Universe is unabashedly celebrating your arrival, it really doesn't matter who else does or doesn't join in the fun.

In a moment I was overcome with a brand new, freshly downloaded version of my narrative. It was one that was infinitely truer than the story I had believed prior. It came from Truth Himself. Anything short of His perspective is an incomplete narrative at best. I had been trying, unsuccessfully, to navigate my life with massive pieces of my identity-map missing. How did I expect to get anywhere? Know where you come from to know where you're going. To successfully arrive at your highest destination, be sure to get your information and directions from the Source.

PRINCIPLE #3: SEEK THE TRUE TRUTH

As St. Paul implores us in Romans 12:2, we are to "...be transformed by the renewing of your mind..." We must allow God to deprogram and reprogram the areas of our minds that hold us back from living fully. The word "renew" means to make new again. Our mind and its thought patterns must be restored to it's original design: healthy, whole, and *Unleashed.*

@thedragonsbutterfly

Pieces of my story, like the reconstructed memory that I just shared, used to cripple me. For example, when I learned about my past and realized that someone literally tried to kill me as an unborn baby, it left me feeling completely unwanted, undesirable, and worthless. I lived with that weight on my shoulders for years. I routinely underachieved because I didn't value my own existence. I made destructive decisions because I didn't care about my life. Now, I look at that same story and come to a completely different conclusion: these people couldn't even kill me when I was 6 months along in the womb! I'm invincible! The same story that held me back my entire life is now what empowers me to live fearlessly, to travel to remote places around the world, to take calculated risks with abandon, and to dare to live fully. I'm completely untouchable until

47

God is done with me. Imagine what that view of reality does to a person.

Suddenly I went from seeing myself as an unwanted, uncelebrated, forgotten child, to understanding that the Creator of the Universe not only knows me, but He's ecstatic at the thought of me being born so that He can be in a communion with me. And when you realize that God Almighty has been protecting you from before you were born, it gives you an unshakable fearlessness way down in your soul, where no human can take it away from you. In this way, God shakes the things that can be shaken "so that what cannot be shaken will remain" (Hebrews 12:27).

The tough times in life can shake us to the core. When we cling to God through trials, though, we come out the other side with profound, unshakable "knowings." It's like panning for gold. After all of the junk is tossed out, we may only be left with one small gold nugget of truth, but it's one that no one can ever take away from us. For example, if you've ever experienced the bliss of seeing God provide for you in impossible ways and coming through for you when there was no other way, you come out of that season of life *knowing* that He's a provider. God as a provider is no longer theory to you. You've moved along on the path from knowing *about* God to *knowing* God. You've tasted and seen that the Lord is good. You've experienced Him and there's no going back from that.

There are a couple of things to note before we continue. First, this technique of seeing God's hand isn't just a way of whitewashing hard memories to avoid dealing with them. Instead, it's a matter of fully facing the real pain and inviting Jesus into that place of pain. Here, we feel and heal at the same time. Second, it's OK (and even

48

good) to be honest with God. You're allowed to say things like, "This sucks. I hate this. It feels awful... And I trust You" all in the same breath. Just read the Psalms and you'll see what I mean. God is big. He can take it when we're real with Him.

By walking through the dark places of our souls, holding on to His capable hand and illuminating these places with His light, we become people of depth who possess stability at the soul-level. Like a well-built ship, we gain weight and strength in the unglamorous and unapplauded territory below the waterline, where our growth isn't apparent to the untrained eye. But this extra weight, this *gravitas*, makes it so that the same little waves don't capsize us anymore. This allows us to navigate even deeper seas, with bigger waves, and a bigger influence in our lives.

As you feel prompted, I invite you to revisit hard memories one by one and ask God where He was when you were going through them. Wait for His response. Allow Him to elevate you and show you His divine perspective. He speaks to everyone in different ways. He may show you a heart-shaped cloud just to let you know that you're loved, or put a meaningful song on the radio, or use a random stranger to tell you that you are, in fact, beautiful, or show you a new version of your story in your mind's eye like He did with me. But listen and look for His response. I dare you. He's pursuing you and wooing you in ways that will only make sense to you.

It may be best to process some of the tough memories with another human you can trust, like a counselor or a mentor. As you journey through your past towards living *Unleashed,* lean on the people in your life who care about you. It helps to have extra support as we journey through these realizations. No one is an island.

The process of getting to wholeness is painful. There is no way to get to the resurrection without going through the crucifixion. It's not easy, but living *Unleashed* is worth the pain of becoming *Unleashed.*

To have God invade your most painful memories, bringing peace, healing, and completeness, it's like this:

"Footprints in the Sand" by Mary Stevenson

One night I dreamed a dream.

As I was walking along the beach with my Lord.

Across the dark sky flashed scenes from my life.

For each scene, I noticed two sets of footprints in the sand,

One belonging to me and one to my Lord.

After the last scene of my life flashed before me,

I looked back at the footprints in the sand.

I noticed that at many times along the path of my life,

especially at the very lowest and saddest times,

there was only one set of footprints.

This really troubled me, so I asked the Lord about it.

"Lord, you said once I decided to follow you,

You'd walk with me all the way.

But I noticed that during the saddest and most troublesome times

Of my life, there was only one set of footprints.

I don't understand why, when I needed You the most,

You would leave me."

He whispered, "My precious child,

I love you and will never leave you

Never, ever, during your trials and testings.

When you saw only one set of footprints,

It was then that I carried you."

REFLECTION:

It's time to use your spiritual imagination:

Where might God have been during my painful memories?

CHAPTER 4

How to Escape from Prison

I've never owned a dog that got fleas. I guess that's because I've never owned a dog. Ideologically I'm not against having a dog as a pet, I just don't really want a dog of my own. I really love other people's dogs, including, and especially, my parents' dog whom my younger brother lovingly named Pepsi. What I love about other peoples' dogs is that I can pet them, take them on walks, and enjoy their company, but at the end of the day they still poop in someone else's backyard, and I can travel without having to think about which poor soul I can convince to take care of them for a week.

Oh right, I was planning to tell you about fleas.

The flea is a remarkable creature. A flea can jump up to 300 times its own height. That's the equivalent of a human jumping the length of three full football fields. Incredible.

Interestingly, though, it's quite easy to limit the achievements of this tiny bundle of potential. All you have to do is take a container and put it on top of the flea for one day. As it jumps it will continue to hit the top of the container over and over. After only a day of this, you can then remove the container and observe a very sad fact. Now, despite the fact that the container is removed, the flea is still only able to jump as high as the limitation you placed on him. It takes the flea several more days to rebuild his strength and get back to jumping as high as he can.

Most of us have no idea how high we can actually jump. For years we've accepted the prison of our limitations, imposed by others or by ourselves, and we haven't bothered to remove the lid. Often when we finally recognize and seek to remove the perceived lid on our lives, our hearts still keeps us jumping at the same level for three common reasons:

1) We can't imagine ourselves going any further.

The true limiting factor, one that happens to be directly within our own spheres of influence and responsibility, is our belief. Now that we've gotten into the habit of living a mediocre, comfortable life, we've stopped dreaming or imagining life looking any different than it is. You won't necessarily achieve every lofty goal you set for your life, but I promise you that you won't reach any purposeful goal that you can't first conceive in your mind's eye as a reality, specifically as reality for you.

2) We've never really pushed the limits.

Push your limits and you'll be surprised to find out that most of them, if not all of them, don't exist at all. Like the flea, we've been living under a self-imposed container, one that dictates and limits what we believe we can accomplish. The entire collection of our limitations exists only in our minds. They're not real. But they feel very real and for years we've convinced ourselves of their reality because now we interpret our circumstances as a confirmation of our biases. Again, we're seeing the world through distorted and tainted lenses and assuming that what we're viewing is fact.

3) We're apathetic because we're afraid.

The fear of failure can grip our souls so deeply that we mistake it for other things. Some of us are so afraid of failing that we've built up defense mechanisms to keep people off of our cases. We've done a great job of pretending we don't really care and that we're just living laid-back lives so that no one questions the real reasons behind our lack of effort and perseverance, and our inability to see anything through to completion. We're afraid of trying and falling flat on our faces, so instead of giving life all we've got we habitually live half-assed existences. That way when we find our life to be completely unfulfilling and we haven't accomplished anything worthwhile, we can say to ourselves with deep, hidden sadness, "Well who cares, I wasn't trying anyway."

If we dig deeper, the roots of these limitations take many forms.

Maybe it was an experience that scarred you deeply; a moment when you let yourself, or someone you love, down terribly. Ever since then, you've believed the lie that you're only capable of hurting the people you love. So you limit yourself, saying that you're not qualified for healthy relationships. This causes you to push people –

who really want to be in your life – away ahead of time so that you don't hurt them.

Maybe someone close to you spoke harsh words over your life. Words are extremely powerful. Maybe they said something like, "You'll never amount to anything" or "you're completely selfish and you never think about anyone else." Though cognitively you might be aware that these statements are untrue, you still haven't convinced your heart.

We have heard it said that "sticks and stones may break my bones but words will never hurt me." That old maxim is B.S. Words have tremendous power. In Proverbs 18:21, King Solomon goes as far as to say that "The tongue holds the power of life and death." With our words, we can change the course of someone's life forever, for good or for bad. Timely words of encouragement can give someone the courage to walk in their destiny. The root of the word "encouragement" is "courage" after all, implying that we have the power to impart courage to someone. "Discouragement" does the exact opposite. It deflates the listener and diminishes their courage. Some awful words spoken into my life from a young age had a subconscious hold on me all the way into my young adult years, when I was finally able to break free using the truth as my key. Furthermore, words spoken by someone meaningful in our lives, like a parent, carry far more weight than words spoken by random people. Knowing that our words hold tremendous power, we must pay close attention to what comes out of our mouths. It could either be life or death, inspiring or killing dreams, depending on what words we choose.

Maybe it was an external circumstance, like the story about hating my birthday. I was given up for adoption as a baby, so for years, based on my lived experience, I limited my life by believing that I wasn't wanted. This belief fuelled many of my detrimental behaviors.

Maybe someone really hurt you. So as a pre-emptive strike, you now choose to hurt people first. That way they can't get to you. Or because someone hurt you - your dad for instance, you're projecting your dad's faults onto how you view God: making Him out to be aloof, or punitive, or a perfectionist (for some examples), when that's not who He is at all. These thoughts patterns can limit your life based on who you believe God to be.

Maybe you're limited by what you think of that one particular affliction, handicap, or dysfunction in your life. You make excuses for what you can accomplish based on this perceived limitation instead of discovering how this stumbling block is giving you superpowers in another area.

I could go on, but here's the point and the fourth principle in living *Unleashed:*

PRINCIPLE #4: REMOVE THE LID

These hindrances will no longer imprison you. No more letting these self-constructed limitations smother your limitless potential. When you come up to another limitation, refuse to accept it as a fatal diagnosis. You will thrive. Keep going.

To break free from these lies, we must consciously and consistently refute every single lie with the truth, one by one. Here's how to tell if the thought is true: does it line up with what God, the Creator of the Universe, says, or not? To know the truth, seek out what He says about you and your circumstances.

If you've believed yourself to be incapable of meaningful relationships, understand that God is love, and He dwells within you.

If, based on people's words, you've believed yourself doomed to a life of mediocrity, again, understand that the Spirit of the Creator of the entire universe dwells within you, so you couldn't possibly be limited.

If you've believed that God is some far-off, unengaged deity, understand that He knows you intimately and wants nothing more than to be in close relationship with you.

If you've believed yourself to be limited by some affliction or circumstances, understand that somehow you have actually been set up for increased success. This is a key to unleashing hidden potential in your life. As we explored earlier, we don't thrive *despite* your limitations; we thrive *because* of our perceived handicaps, especially when these limitations are placed in God's strong and capable hands.

> *"Whether you think you can or whether you think you can't, you're right."* ~ Henry Ford

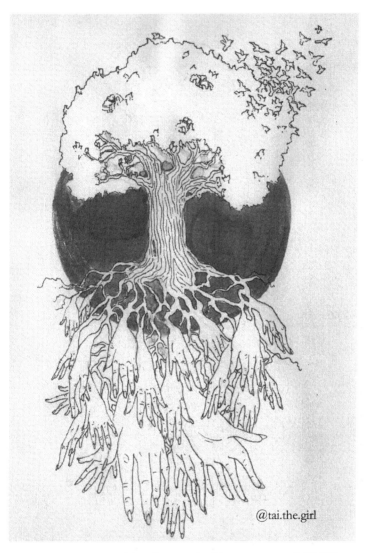

@tai.the.girl

I'm pretty sure that I'd be diagnosed with some sort of ADHD or another learning disorder if I actually got tested. Instead of belittling myself as easily distracted, I've learned to celebrate my super-human amounts of energy and tremendous capacity to connect the dots even when there are a bunch of moving pieces. Furthermore, I've built systems around me to help maintain focus even when I don't feel like it. This way I can enjoy the benefits that come with my disposition while alleviating the downside. And I leave a lot of room for grace.

It is not enough to expose the lies. We have to replace the lies with the truth to break free and live *Unleashed*.

You may not recognize the name Gillian Lynne, but you are probably familiar with her work. She choreographed two of the most celebrated and longest-running Broadway shows of all time, namely *Cats* and *The Phantom of the Opera*. When she was young, Gillian's school became troubled by her disruptive presence. The school wrote to her parents saying they thought she had a learning disability because she had an incredibly difficult time concentrating in class. Her mother, concerned, brought her to a doctor and explained what was going on to find out what was wrong with her. After listening, the doctor told Gillian that he'd like to step out to speak to her mother privately and they would be back very soon. As the two were leaving the room the room, the doctor turned on the radio on his desk, and they walked out. Once they exited the room and looked in through the window, they saw that Gillian was up on her feet, moving to the music. After observing for a few moments, the doctor turned to the mother and said, "Mrs. Lynne, your daughter isn't sick. She's a dancer."[5]

[5] Ken Robinson – Ted Talk
https://www.ted.com/talks/ken_robinson_says_schools_kill_creativity

> *"Above all else, to thine own self be true."*
> ~ *William Shakespeare*

With all of my blatant deficiencies, I lived thinking there was something seriously wrong with me. But as it turns out, I'm not broken and I'm not sick. I'm an entrepreneur. I'm an artist. I'm a revolutionary.

Struggling to squeeze myself into the appropriate societal boxes growing up was awful. To this day, I still have to fight against the desire to water myself down so that I can just fit in. I have to consistently remind myself of how terrible an experience it was when I tried being normal once; it was the worst 30 seconds of my life.

Our society unwittingly punishes people for being anything other than the compliant worker bees that grow up to become an effective consumer. It starts in school. No matter our energy level or personal ways of learning, we are most often expected to sit down, be quiet, and pay attention while we're lectured to. Imagine (for some this may not be farfetched) that you had to endure that as an adult for eight hours per day. You sit down. Someone talks at you. And then you're supposed to respond by continuing to be quiet and apply your knowledge on a sheet of paper. Only a small percentage of our children are wired to learn this way, yet this is the expectation for all. Children that don't fit this learning style we demean as below average or label them with a disorder and place them in a less advanced program.

> *"Everyone is a genius. But if you judge a fish by its ability to climb a tree, it will live its whole life believing that it is stupid."*
>
> *~ Albert Einstein*

Your particular affliction becomes an asset when it is properly engaged. Your apparent weaknesses give you super-powers in other areas.

In saying this, it is still important for us to know our weaknesses, to be honest with our shortcomings, and to build structures and accountability in those areas so that they do not become liabilities to us and to others. There is freedom in knowing who you are and who you are not, and in relying on God's grace as He somehow uses your feeble attempts for His glory.

Develop your strengths and mitigate your weaknesses. Don't apologize for possessing qualities that you should be labeling as gifts. And don't ignore your struggles because they may contain clues to your destiny.

REFLECTION:

The question is not, "Am I a genius?" but rather, "What is my genius?"

CHAPTER 5

How to Find Your Car Keys

Let's go deeper still.

I was out for a leisurely stroll on a brisk fall night. The air was crisp at that perfect level that makes the nerves in your face feel like they're dancing but not hurting. In the distance, I noticed a man on his hands and knees crawling around under the light of a street lamp. As I approached, it was clear that he was meticulously searching for something seemingly quite important.

"Excuse me, Sir," I asked, "Is everything alright?"

"Yes I'm fine, I just looking for my lost car keys."

"Oh, let me help!"

"Awesome, I would really appreciate that."

So I got down on my hands and knees to look around under the light of this street lamp. Very quickly I had scoured the small circle of light and there definitely wasn't a set of keys there at all. So I asked, "Are you sure you lost your keys here?"

"No, I lost them in my front yard" he replied, "but this is where the light is so I'm looking here instead."

This is not a true story; it is an allegory reminding us that we don't often find the truth in well-lit places. So in this chapter, we will spend some time exploring the darkness, not just where the light is, to uncover the paradigms that hold us back from living *Unleashed*. Let's go deeper.

I'm about to reveal a vulnerable piece of my journey as an example of how we shape our reality. A friend of mine and gifted listener, Kevin, led me through a powerful activity that drastically changed my universe, laying the trail of breadcrumbs out for me beautifully on the way to a major breakthrough.

The reflection started with a simple question, "What's holding you back?" I began to list out some of my frustrations while he took notes. My answers were: a lack of time, a lack of energy, a lack of focus, a lack of zeal for life, a lack of resources, a lack of support from key people in my life... and on I went.

"Great," Kevin remarked, "what do you notice about the items on this list?"

After some guided discussion, we concluded together that we could easily classify the bulk of what I had named under the category of "circumstances." Lack of time is a circumstance, lack of energy is a circumstance, and so on.

"So," he continued, "you and I both know that your circumstances aren't the real problem. Circumstances are what we find in the light, it's what's easy for us to see, and easy for us to use as a scapegoat, blaming our outcomes on abstract thoughts or on other people. Let's go deeper still... What are you doing or not doing, as in which actions are you taking or not taking, that causes these circumstances?"

Hmm, it's starting to get uncomfortable. What are the actions that I have to take responsibility for? For example, I am not late because of traffic or some external circumstance. If I'm late, it's because I mismanaged my time.

What's the cause of a lack of time and energy and focus in my life? As I pondered, I took inventory of my habits, like the habit of procrastination, among other unhealthy ones I had developed. Most remarkably I took note of the fact that I was routinely saying "yes" to too many things that didn't matter, and "no" to things that were quite beneficial to me. This is a habit I refer to as "superman syndrome". It's the need to be needed by others and to be perceived as competent.

Obviously, saying "yes" to too many things leads to some terrible ends. It caused me to drop the ball on important tasks, to let others down routinely. This habit damaged my reputation, left me feeling burned out and low on energy, and consistently stressed by the apparent lack of time in a day to accomplish everything I "needed" to do. I was scatterbrained and without focus, doing a lot and accomplishing very little.

"Well, we can both see that this way of living clearly isn't working for you. So why on earth are you still doing it? Why, if a person knows in his or her mind that something doesn't work, would anyone continue to travel down the same path?" Kevin started, "So let's go deeper… What thought, idea or belief do you hold about yourself or others that would cause you, as your default, to say 'yes' to things you know you clearly shouldn't say 'yes' to?"

> *"The definition of insanity is doing the same thing over and over and expecting different results." ~ Albert Einstein*

I wanted to end the cycle of insanity, so I was willing to wade through the mire of rawness and pain. I journeyed deeper.

The thought that came to mind almost brought me to tears. "I feel like I'm not enough," I said, "I say 'yes' to things I shouldn't because I feel like I'm not enough and that I have something to prove. I think the idea stems from the story I've believed, subconsciously, about being given up for adoption at birth. In my mind, I wasn't wanted so I feel like I have to prove to the world that I deserve to be here, to prove that the world would be worse off without me. I'm trying to justify my existence and prove my worth."

Major breakthrough.

"Now," Kevin continued, "imagine how your life would be different if you operated within the understanding that you are enough, just the way you are and without doing anything at all."

"Well for starters," I said, "I wouldn't be over-promising and under-delivering on my commitments because I wouldn't have anything to prove. I would do a lot less and do it well. If I attended a function, my motivation would be real desire or true commitment, rather than an obligation or the fear of letting people down. My life would look much different."

FULL.

AND I WONDER IF THE MOON UNDERSTANDS ITS
BEAUTY OR IF IT EVEN KNOWS OR CARES
AT ALL.

@tai.the.girl

Since then, I've been captivated by the idea of living life out of a place of abundance, knowing in my "knower," not simply in my mind, that I AM ENOUGH – just the way I am, and for no other reason than my just being here.

We can find our deeper motivations by traveling a path similar to the following sentences. Start with 'this is my circumstance'. Move to 'these are the actions that caused those circumstances'. And finally, go into the deep waters of 'these are the ideas/beliefs about myself, others, or the world that fuelled those actions'. That way we can uncover what truly caused those circumstances.

It's tough to get out of a rut. A rut is formed by walking consistently on a familiar path, usually over the span of many years, and sometimes over the span of multiple generations. A rut is a well-worn path due to repetitive travel. With frequent use, it becomes increasingly difficult to travel outside of the rut. We've worn a divot into the ground, making it much easier to sink back into it than it is to take the high road.

"Hmm… and how's that working for you?"

~ my wife

We all have conditioned patterns of thinking, and by proxy, patterns of behaving, which ultimately form our circumstances. These patterns are our default, especially under pressure or stress. Fortunately and unfortunately, a path is the only way to move forward. I say "fortunately" because we have the power to, through ceaseless importunity, form new, healthy, patterns of thinking by choosing thoughts that are pure, right, lovely, admirable, and praiseworthy. We can renew our minds. I also say "unfortunately" because as we've seen, the work required to move forward is typically more uncomfortable than staying where we are, at least in the short-term.

In order to recondition our lives, we must recognize the unhealthy thoughts and choose to dwell on righteous thoughts until operating in the Divine becomes second nature. After some time, it becomes harder to do the wrong thing than it is to do the right thing, all through the disciplined conditioning of our habits. Put in the hard work of forming and maintaining the right paths, and soon these paths will become your default, even and especially under pressure.

> *"The issue is rarely the issue." ~ Unknown*

For many of us, the fruit our life produces is discouraging. By "fruit", I'm referring to the ongoing results and outcomes. We hate when we burst out in anger, or when we give in to the same addiction, or when we pretend to be someone we're not at an event. You name it. These are examples of fruit. And we go into cycles of activity where we're determined to rid our lives of this nasty fruit. So we go fruit picking. We use all of our energy to remove the rotten fruit from our lives. We pick as much of it as we can see, and we throw it far away. But even if we managed to get rid of all of the bad fruit, within a short time we're back to producing the same results in our lives. The problem, then, can't just be the fruit. There is a problem with the tree itself. We have to go down deep into the roots to discover why our tree keeps producing those results. Fruit picking will not change what your tree produces. The whole tree must be redeemed in order for it to produce a different result.

PRINCIPLE #5: GET TO THE ROOT

Our broken patterns of thinking run deeper than we know. Here's what happens if you chain a baby elephant by the foot to a wooden pole (which you should never do, but the idea serves as a helpful example). If the chain is five feet long, the elephant lives the first few years of its life walking around within a five-foot radius. Amazingly, once that chain is removed a few years later, the elephant will remain within that same five-foot radius for a long time. It has now accepted its conditioned limitations, though the limitation no longer exists in reality at all.

The saying "an elephant never forgets" is true for a few reasons. Elephants are great at remembering their migration paths. They're great at knowing exactly who is in their herd and who is an outsider posing a threat to their safety. But this tremendous aptitude for remembering can also be a disadvantage. When they are in captivity, their incredible memories condition the elephants to remember their oppression for far too long. They remain in mental bondage even when they are physically free.

Most of us are living life in mental, emotional, and spiritual chains. To live *Unleashed*, we must remove the chains that hold us, but more than this, we actually have to fight hard to maintain our freedom. It takes even more work to live like a free person once the chains are gone. Disturbingly, many prisoners of war, once liberated, will run back to the place of captivity out of mere familiarity. They default back to their unhealthy situations out of comfort. Get out and stay out. Often, staying free requires us to have a community of support around us, especially while we're seeking to break out of patterns that have held us captive for a long time.

We are responsible for most outcomes in our lives, as we create these outcomes via the thought patterns we maintain and the actions that follow. Sure, there are many situations upon which we can try to confer blame, but freedom is found through the path of truth. You and I must vehemently and continually oppose the comfortable yet destructive habit of pointing fingers at other people or events as the cause of our current realities. We need to spend time uprooting and destroying any inkling of this pattern in our own hearts if we want to walk the pathways of peace and fulfillment.

We may be holding on to what someone has done to us, or the cards we've been dealt by virtue of our origins, or any other excuses for that matter. It is true that many of these circumstances were and are, largely, outside of our control. You're not to blame for what happened to you, but you are responsible for what you choose to do as your life's reply. Life is a conversation. What someone else does is only, at most, half of the dialogue. What will you say back, with your words and actions, and with how you choose to live your life?

No one else in the entire world, except you, has any control over your *response* to circumstances or your *mindset* moving forward. These are areas no one can touch without your consent. Thus, you must recognize your full responsibility for any ongoing circumstances in direct relation to your mindset. Understanding this fact is humbling and sobering. But even more, understanding this fact is empowering and exhilarating. We have the power to change our world.

We, through our thoughts, eventually but surely create our realities. If your reality doesn't line up with your thoughts, you need only to spend more time going in that direction. If you've maintained a strong, industrious, and positive outlook and still haven't reaped the fruit of those thoughts, keep going. A seed must produce the precise tree contained within. An apple seed cannot produce a dandelion, no matter how hard it tries. Time will not prove to be a liar. We always reap what we sow. Consistently degrade your thoughts and you have degraded your life. Consistently elevate your thoughts and you have elevated your life.

Beliefs fuel thoughts. Thoughts fuel actions. Actions fuel circumstances. Circumstances fuel beliefs. On and on the cycle continues, either for better or for worse. To live *Unleashed* we must go deeper still.

REFLECTION:

You, too, can undertake this soul-searching activity on your own time. The progression is simple: work your way from looking at your circumstances to the actions that fuel them, to the dominating (often unconscious) thoughts that fuel your actions. Write down your answers to the following questions in this order:

Step 1: What's holding me back?

Step 2: What actions am I doing that cause those circumstances?

Step 3: What idea is fuelling those actions? What inaccurate idea do I believe about myself, others, God?

CHAPTER 6

How to Give Up

The shirt you wore when you were a child isn't necessarily a bad shirt altogether. It served a purpose at that time. I look back at some of my childhood photos and am extremely thankful that my mom, for the most part, chose timeless pieces like turtleneck sweaters, with which to clothe me. When revisiting the old photos later in life, I found the oversized, square glasses I wore as a toddler to be fashionably problematic, but everything comes back around eventually. Now, as I sit here writing and enjoying the flavors of a delicious Burundi pour-over coffee in a hip coffee shop, there are several skinny-jeaned, plaid-shirt-wearing fellows with very large spectacles upon their faces. I don't see myself going back to wearing this style, but the ebbs and flows of fashion bring me some level of comfort. I now know that I cannot possibly miss the mark, I risk only finding myself ahead of the times.

Initially there was a point to that monologue. The shirt isn't bad; it just doesn't fit anymore. As you begin living *Unleashed*, pursuing your life's calling and renouncing any limitations which hold you back, you'll notice that you become increasingly uncomfortable with any behaviors and activities that don't advance the mission.

The things we used to do aren't all wrong. Eventually, though, you will find that certain people, places, behaviors, and things just don't fit with where you are. They especially don't fit with where you're heading. As the Master reminds us, quoted in Matthew 9:17, we can't "pour new wine into old wineskins." New wine would crack the old wineskin and the old wineskin would adversely affect the flavor of the wine. Newness demands newness. Every new level of life demands a new you.

Last chapter we discussed how to let go of negative thought patterns and behaviors. Here we're going to look at two more things we need to learn to give up when they are no longer beneficial: some relationships and some environments.

The following are some lessons I learned from a tree. Not everyone who started the journey with you will finish the journey with you. Healthy relationships – personal, business, or otherwise – all rely on clearly defined and consistently upheld expectations. We run into trouble when we try to be something we're not, or when we try to make other people something they're not. I have found the analogy of a tree helpful in identifying three basic – and oversimplified for the purpose of our exploration – types of relationships. People can either be leaves, branches, or roots in our lives.

The leaf:

A leaf is great for a season. It comes into your life at just the right time, adding capacity, shade, and beauty to your world. When the wind blows too hard, or when the sun gets too hot, or when the weather changes from summer to autumn, leaves naturally fall off.

They lose their lustre and gently fall to the ground. These are people whom God brings into our lives for a specific time and purpose, but not for long. When it's time, we must allow them to fall to make way for new growth.

The branch:

A branch is much more solid than a leaf. Branches grow with you through the years. It would take a tremendous wind or natural disaster to break off a well-established branch. These branches remain steadfast through almost all changes in the weather. They reach upwards towards your goals with you. They help bear the weight of many burdens. At some point, though, several branches will inevitably become obsolete. Perhaps the unusually heavy weight of a particular burden caused them to break under the pressure. Maybe a disease or pest caused the branch to rot from the inside out, making it toxic to the tree. Sometimes even solid branches can break, for whatever reasons. And sometimes, branches will remain solid through the entire lifespan of the tree. These are people upon whom you can rely, but not always indefinitely. Lean on them, but know that it is possible for them to break under too much pressure.

The root:

A root is part of the tree's foundation. Roots go deep, unaffected by any changes in the weather. In fact, they stabilize the tree in order to give it additional grounding during trying times. The roots are committed to searching out nutrition and sustenance, anything to help the tree thrive. Roots are often unseen, and usually under-appreciated. They're steady like the sun. They're not constantly looking for attention or approval. They just are. Only the death of the tree or intentional sabotage could kill a well-developed root system. These are the people who work their ways into the core of our beings, who love us with an unshakeable love, who are connected to us at the soul level. These people are family – whether by blood or not. Keep in mind that not everyone who is related by blood is necessarily family. You won't *like* the roots at all times, and you don't have to, because you love them and they love you. You may even lose touch with someone who is part of your root system for years, but they are still part of your foundation.

We would do well to stop trying to force people to be someone they are not. When people show you who they are, believe them. There are some leaves in our lives that we try to force into being a part of our root system. That doesn't work. Conversely, there are some people who should be a part of our root system whom we try to keep at a distance, pretending they're expendable, despite their authenticity and consistency. That doesn't work either. It may just be that the person rubs you the wrong way because her presence and feedback challenge you to be better, and that makes you uncomfortable. He or she could still be a root in your life.

> *"The important thing is this: to be able at any moment to sacrifice what we are for what we could become."*
> ~ *Charles Dubois*

Nature is a wonderful teacher when we are paying attention. After learning from trees, let's consider what we can learn from a lobster. The adult lobster sheds its shell and grows a new shell about once a year. The stimulus for the lobster to change is that he has grown to the point where living in his current shell has become excruciating. In fact, he has reached the point of growth where it would be far more painful for him to maintain the status quo than it would be for him to take the agonizing next steps towards transformation. He is bumping up against the limits of his environment, so he must change. To do this, he goes under a rock for protection, sheds his shell, and painfully produces a new one. He emerges from under the rock liberated from his old self and with further room to grow over the coming months.

There comes a time during the growth process where our old shells – old circles of friends, old stomping-grounds, old events – don't serve our evolution any longer. To grow, we must go. You do so humbly and quietly, knowing that this season of your life, as you know it, has come to end. There is no need to let your former shell know why you can't stay there. You have only to act. It is painful to shed your comfort, your limitations, and to dare to live greatly. At some point, it becomes more painful for you to stay where you are. You have limited time on this earth. There isn't a moment to waste.

"Teach us to number our days that we may gain a heart of wisdom." ~ Psalm 90:12

There are times when even our presence may be holding others back from growth as well. If we are always there to fill leadership gaps, we may be preventing another leader from discovering more within him or her than that person knows. Or if we co-dependently enable someone to continue in his or her destructive behavior, we are doing more harm than good.

PRINCIPLE #6: GIVE UP ON
THE RIGHT THINGS

It is important to note that we are not to simply give up on people and places when things get hard. There is a big difference between quitting prematurely out of a lack of perseverance, and letting go when it is actually time to do so. We are to let go of the unhealthy parts, not the challenging ones. Also, know that you may find yourself in a situation whereby it is let go of an unhealthy dynamic within a relationship, but not the relationship itself.

In the same way, our immune systems, when functioning properly, rid our bodies of disease, we must make time to pay attention to our mental, emotional, and spiritual immune systems to know what is contributing positively or negatively to our well being. For example, we don't leave our marriages because they are difficult, but we do give up on the negative patterns of interacting within our marriages. Changing our toxic relationships in these cases could mean the opposite of leaving. Growth in this instance may look like doing the hard work of transforming our current relationships instead of seeking new ones. In the case of marital abuse, however, setting strong boundaries or even physically leaving the person may be the path towards transformation for both parties.

As we learned in the previous chapters, this is not a matter of running away from pain. Instead, this is a matter of shedding unnecessary weight. What do you need to give up to get to where you're going? A heavy backpack overstocked with supplies, even some good supplies, could be the thing keeping you from getting to the top of a mountain. Take with you only what is necessary for the journey.

> *"Let us throw off every weight that slows us down and the sin that so easily trips us up. And let us run with endurance the race God has set before us…"* ~ *Hebrews 12:1*

Your destiny matters. It's time to move forward and it will require you to (prayerfully) let go of some things in order to do so.

"He who would accomplish little need sacrifice little.
 He who would achieve much must sacrifice much.
 He who would attain highly must sacrifice greatly."
 ~ James Allen

REFLECTION:

Put everything on the table for inspection.

What must I let go of to move forward?

CHAPTER 7

How to Get a Life

Most of us aren't terribly lost. We've just wandered off the path a bit. Some have drifted more than others. Some of us can still see the path from where we are. Some of us have gone so far that we have no idea in which direction the path could possibly be by now. And some of us have never walked (at least consciously or intentionally) on anything that looks like a meaningful path. Living *Unleashed,* finding true fulfillment on our journeys, requires a return to our true paths and continual realignment to stay there.

Lost is not a geographical location; it's a state of the soul. You may discover – in searching the dark recesses of the heart – that you are indeed lost right within your own home, within your own skin. The real problem is that until you know that you're lost, you cannot possibly hope to find your way.

There are far too many aimless wanderers and not enough adventurers.

I love all of my hippie friends. Sometimes they share inspirational quotes on social media that make me feel all warm and fuzzy inside, like: "Not all who wander are lost." That line, taken from J.R.R. Tolkien's poem "All That is Gold Does Not Glitter" is usually posted with a great photo of some cool person standing beside a gorgeous waterfall with the jungle as the backdrop.

And this is true; not *all* who wander are lost. There are certainly times on our journey where some unchartered exploring is exactly what we need in order to find our way. But let's be honest, lots of us who wander are most definitely and completely lost. It only takes one nice little quote spun the wrong way to justify our current reality when sometimes we are, in fact, truly aimless. When taken too literally and in the absence of a commitment to brutally honest introspection, sayings such as the aforementioned can cause us to stop asking the tough, soul-probing questions that can lead to the discovery of a peace-filled, abundant life.

Exploring and wandering are two very different actions, but they look dangerously similar. Curiosity and stupidity are also distant cousins. As with most things, there is a healthy tension between each of these ideas. Tension isn't a bad thing; tension is what holds everything in balance. The closer we get to the line where the ideas meet, though, the harder it is to tell which is which. The worst is when we're lost but we're convinced that we're adventuring. It's much like one of my favorite John Maxwell maxims on leadership: "He that thinketh he leadeth, and hath no one following, is only taking a walk."

There exists a complicated algorithm to determine whether you're on an adventure or just lost. I'll give it to you for you to use on yourself, for your own benefit, as often as you wish. It's a formula that you can use at any point on your journey to check in. You might want to get out your calculator before we start. Here it goes:

Step 1: Make a mental inventory of where you are and what you're currently doing with your precious time here on earth.

Step 2: Ask yourself *"why?"*

Step 3: Either have a good answer or discover the noticeable absence of a good answer.

Step 4: The end.

If you can't answer with a meaningful and/or compelling 'why,' you might be lost. Your 'why' doesn't need to be complicated, but it needs to be present. What you are currently doing should contribute, in some small or large way, to your overall purpose in life.

Keep in mind I'm not asking you to answer me, or anyone else in your life for that matter. I'm asking you to answer, honestly, your own soul while it inquires of you. You may be able to convince everyone else that you're living life directly within the apex of your purpose, but you certainly can't lie to God and you can't lie to yourself. Why, truly, are you here? If you can't answer that question yet, don't worry. That's the point of us spending this time together. Remember, we're digging deep because the world needs you to be the best version of yourself.

If you find yourself deep in the wilderness, that's not necessarily a problem. If you're in the wilderness and you don't at least know why you're there, where you're headed, or how you got to where you are... big problem. That means you're lost.

Allow me to make an important distinction before you get overwhelmed. Living on purpose does not mean that you have your whole life in order or that you have everything figured out. It simply means that you have something definite and meaningful to aim at.

> *"The glory of God is man fully alive."* ~ *St. Irenaeus*

Simply stated, living in your purpose is the gift of knowing why you're here. It's the art of living with compelling vision and a worthwhile pursuit, of seeing the faint, sometimes barely-perceivable outline of a mountaintop way in the distance, and setting your course towards the peak. It is keeping the image of that distant goal in mind even when you are treading through the muck and mire of the valleys, where the only distinguishable thing is complete darkness. It is continually, and unashamedly, readjusting your trajectory every time you get a glimpse of that mountain to make sure you maintain the course. Purpose is seeing the goal always, although sometimes only in your mind's eye.

Purpose is not, however, the full roadmap. It does not tell you exactly what you will encounter on the way to your destination: the unexpected challenges you'll have to overcome, the rocky terrain that you'll be under-equipped to cross, the weather and the elements outside of your control. Herein lies the adventure.

With nothing to aim at, you cannot possibly know whether you're getting any closer to your real goal. Consider how impossible it is to establish meaningful checkpoints along the way without an overall understanding of where you want to end up.

Imagine that you're climbing a very tall ladder. In the beginning, the climb is fairly easy, but about a quarter of the way up you start to feel your muscles burning a bit. You find the strength to press on when your arms get heavy and weak. You are exerting all of your energy. You ignore the pain and even learn to cherish the sweat and scars brought on by the intense process. You're making progress, rung by rung. Your foot may slip a little from time to time, but you never stop moving upward. The people on the ground are cheering for you and telling you not to give up. And finally, when you feel like you have nothing left to give, you get a glimpse of the top of the ladder. This gives you the courage to continue on. Then, the glorious arrival: you reach the top. Once you catch your breath, you stand up and turn around to enjoy your accomplishment... only to realize that you had accidentally placed your ladder up against the wrong building.

That is how many ambitious people live their lives. This is why effort and persistence are not enough. If you're heading in the wrong direction, running harder actually gets you further from where you want to go. It's sobering to realize that it is quite easy for us to zealously spend many of our precious breaths, our energy and resources, on a completely worthless pursuit.

> *"Our greatest fear should not be of failure, but of succeeding at something that doesn't really matter."* ~ D.L. Moody

From a lack of purpose comes the mid-life, or any-point-in-life, crisis. When weighing your life, you realize that you've spent all of these years running on a hamster wheel and it hasn't brought you true fulfillment. At this point, many people start to grope around in the dark at their immediate surroundings, looking for something within their grasp with which they try to fill the chasm in their soul. We reason with ourselves: I must need a new car. Or a new job. Or a new spouse.

The problem with this approach is that we're trying to change the outside without changing the inside at all. It's like putting a vibrant, brand-new orange peel on top of a pungent, rotten orange. No matter what you change in terms of your circumstances, if your heart and soul don't change, you'll find yourself dealing with the same deep loneliness and dissatisfaction as before, maybe even on a larger scale now that you've sabotaged important things in your effort to fix things yourself.

No matter how many years you've lived, the key is to have a healthy internal crisis as often as needed to stay on track. Be willing to ask yourself the hard questions and don't take the comfortable way out, simply trying to change your circumstances. We were created to live for something beyond ourselves. Until we find that, our meaningless toiling under the sun will amount to nothing and we will never find deep fulfillment.

PRINCIPLE #7: AIM AT WHAT MATTERS

Ask yourself what really matters. Then have the courage to build your whole life around your answer.

It takes tremendous courage to live from your soul instead of responding to your own fears or other peoples' opinions of what they think is best for you. Counsel is good. Leaning on the wisdom of others is good. But at the end of our lives, we, alone, will be accountable for the actions we chose. No one else has to answer to

God for the way you lived your life. People can, and should, help direct your path to make sure you're staying on track. But they cannot walk the path for you.

So, who are you, really?

We are called human *beings* for a reason. It's important, then, to note that success has nothing to do with what we do. Success is found in *being* who we were created to be and allowing all of our *doing* to flow from that profound wellspring of life. A cup was created to hold liquid. It can do many other things, but its ideal purpose remains the same. You can do many things, but your purpose remains the same. Who are you? Based on the answer to that question, you can begin the process of discovering what you were truly created to do. Don't let the idea of "human being" give you an excuse to be lazy, though. We have got to be taking action, and doing so with zeal and passion. The difference here is that the 'doing' should be spilling out of who we are.

Most of us live life believing the idea:
I do, therefore, I am.

That's backwards.
I am, therefore I do.

Generally I enjoy messing with people, but especially so when I'm meeting someone for the first time. After shaking hands and exchanging names, I don't like to ask the other person what they do.

What a silly question anyway. When people ask that question, what they're really asking is "what do you do to earn money?" so that they can get some clues as to where you fit in the societal pecking order. Instead, I usually ask something like, "What are you all about? What's your passion?" Most people are caught off guard and still answer me by saying that they're the VP of Sales at such-and-such important place, which is fine, but it's not really what I'm after. I'd rather have them say, "I love helping people, so I currently do that as the VP of such-and-such place." Next time someone asks you what you do at some lame networking session, I challenge you to answer him or her with your passion instead. And ask what they're passionate about. I find it lays the foundation for a much richer conversation. Either that or people look at you like you're from another planet and slowly walk away.

If you don't know exactly who you really are, I have some good news for you. No one fully does. But there are people who seek and follow God's breadcrumb clues along the path and who have tapped into the deeper places of their identities. We are all on a lifelong journey of becoming more and more 'us'.

The answer you're looking for is not complicated. Life is simple. It's not easy, but it is simple.

As for me, I tend to have a fairly large existential crisis at least once a month. It was during one of these times of internal anguish, questioning the meaning of life and my purpose on the planet, that I came across an idea that has changed my life forever. Here is a simple guideline for discovering your life's purpose, your calling, amidst the glaring voices of society and your own selfish interests.

Frederick Buechner, in his book *Wishful Thinking*, draws attention to the fact that the English word "vocation" is derived from the Latin word "vocare," which means 'to call'. Vocation, then, is not the same thing as our work, our job, or our career. Those may be ways in which we fulfill our calling, but none of those is our calling. Work is the stuff we do to get things done. A job happens to be a place where we can do work. A career is an overall pattern of many jobs strung together. But a vocation is a life mission; one that informs all of the other areas mentioned.

In following this train of thought, having a "calling" presumes a caller. And this caller is the living God Himself. Here's Buechner's insightful recommendation on how to search for our purpose, our calling:

> "By and large a good rule for finding out is this: the kind of work God usually calls you to is the kind of work (a) that you need most to do and (b) that the world most needs to have done... **The place God calls you to is the place where your deep gladness and the world's deep hunger meet**"[6]

A good way to think about calling, Buechner suggests, is that your calling lives at the intersection of your *deep gladness* and the world's *deep hunger*. Finding your true purpose necessitates both a look inward and a look outward. Who am I? And how can I engage who I am towards making the world a better place?

[6] http://www.calledthejourney.com/blog/2014/12/17/frederick-buechner-on-calling

This idea contains a beautiful simplicity. This is the intersection to look for. What brings your soul deep gladness? Is it dancing? Writing? What would you do for free? OK, great, now how can you use that to make someone's life better? How can you use who you are to serve the people within your reach? It could be as simple as the fact that you love being with people and listening to their stories. Awesome! Go use that gift to heal this broken world. You could hang out in a seniors' center and give them the tremendous gift of a listening ear so they can share their wisdom.

Note that this intersection is not an exact location, but rather a tool to reorient the compass of our life towards the continual pursuit of the worthwhile. Over time, your passions will evolve to encompass different areas of life, and they will intersect with the needs of humanity in different ways as you go along. The key is to find sustainable ways to live at this juncture as much as possible. We'll see in a later chapter how our gifts and talents can also factor into our understanding of our life's calling.

Furthermore, there is deep fulfillment available to us through the mastery of our craft. We can gain deep happiness not from being in the 'perfect' roles, but rather by gaining expertise in our domains through discipline. Even in the mundane areas of life, like washing dishes, we can find internal bliss by practicing intentionality and presence, which manifests in the wholehearted excellence of our current undertakings. Again, our 'doing' is subservient to our 'being'.

If you aim at nothing, you'll hit it every time. Much of our personal dissatisfaction stems from aimlessness, but once we get past that, we are likely to meet another joy-killer on the path: unmet expectations.

The gap between where we are and where we want to be can cause a tremendous amount of angst. The key to overcome this form of depression is to celebrate the steps rather than the destination. The need to have everything all at once prevents us from having anything at all. This is because we give up too easily when life doesn't look exactly as we want it to.

If we were trying to lose weight, most of us wouldn't be satisfied with losing one pound per week (which is a healthy rate of progress) when we want to lose a total of twenty pounds. We want all twenty pounds gone at once. And so we become discouraged and quit our healthy lifestyles when we don't see the results as fast as we want them. Or we lose the weight too quickly but haven't actually changed our daily habits at all, so the weight comes back right away.

When we learn to measure our progress by whether or not we're taking the small actions that get us there, it takes the pressure off of the massive expectations we have for our lives. Ironically, walking the path step by step is the only possible way to reach the lofty goals anyway.

I define success much differently now. I was led to a profound realization one day while sitting in a café drinking an Americano with a phenomenal business-coach. He said, "It seems to me that you're expending a tremendous amount of time and energy towards 'achieving success.'" I took this as an encouragement, but I soon realized that he had set me up when he proceeded to ask me a couple of simple, earth-shattering questions. "But what does the word 'success' actually mean to you? And how will you know when you've reached it?"

I had no idea how to answer that question. Posturing, I fumbled my way through a completely gutless answer while his eyes glared right into my soul through the veil of my pretend confidence. I realized that I had no idea what I even meant when I said 'success'. Ouch. I was spinning my tires in life, using lots of gas, making a lot of noise, and going nowhere meaningful at all.

Since then, I've had to wrestle through what a 'successful' life looks like for me. And in my contemplation, I received an answer that helped point me towards a much more meaningful question.

From my understanding, success is nothing more, and nothing less, than achieving the purpose for which a person was sent. That's it.

So in looking at true success through that lens, it leads us back to our existential question: why am I here? The only way to measure success accurately is to use our life's purpose as the canon. Success is for me to be who I am meant to be, to the full measure, and in a way that advances God's Kingdom. To succeed, I have to be who I am, fully. It's so simple. It's not easy, but it's simple.

Success has nothing to do with how much money you have in your bank account. It has nothing to do with your social status, or which letters you have behind your name. God has placed you here, with your unique wiring, skills, and abilities, to achieve a very specific purpose. Fulfilling your purpose IS success. Now, to pick on money as an example because many of us humans are obsessed with using it as a measurement tool, your purpose *may* include a calling to use wealth to make a make a massive difference in the lives of others, but true purpose cannot be captured by the accumulation of dollars. A better measure, when it comes to finances, is how we use money to advance the cause of justice. Conversely, the fulfillment of your purpose may include a vow of financial poverty in order to gain greater spiritual wealth because money has been a vice for you in the past. There is no one-size-fits-all definition of success because each of us is created uniquely.

> "Nobody is superior. Nobody is inferior. But nobody is equal
> either. People are simply unique, incomparable.
> You are you. I am I." ~ Osho

Again, success is achieving the purpose for which you were sent. A successful cup is one that holds liquid well, not one that is great at hammering nails into a wall. To discover our truest purposes, we must ferociously resist our human tendencies towards comparison. Your life journey is identical to no one else's and therefore your progress cannot be measured against someone else's journey. You may look to others for clues. By looking at someone else's life, you may discover principles of what to do (or what not to do) if they've already walked a path similar to the one you're currently on or would like to be on. But you still cannot measure your life by someone else's version of success. This is an emotional boundary that I find exceptionally hard to maintain in the era of social media. Comparison is a mortal enemy of true fulfillment.

God's opinion of our life is the only one that matters. And he doesn't measure our lives by our achievements, as we humans are prone to do. He measures success strictly by our obedience in following Him, not by the results we obtain. Did you do what He asked you to do? Did you use the gifts He gave you to advance His Kingdom of love and right-living? Our job is to hear Him and obey Him. We leave the results to Him. Though following Him definitely takes us on a difficult and the narrow path, it takes a tremendous amount of pressure off of our shoulders when we realize that He is responsible for the results of our obedience.

> *"Very few are meant for a life of notoriety, yet all of us are meant for a life of significance. We should never confuse fame with greatness."* ~ Erwin McManus

We can achieve greatness without fame. And we can become famous without ever living great lives. All of us are called to live significant lives, even though what may seem like an insignificant calling. There is tremendous power available to us when we realize that each of our actions is incredibly significant, down to the smallest of deeds. Here I'm reminded of Mother Theresa's famous line as she reminds us that "we can do no great things, only small things with great love."

The key to getting anywhere is to set your destination first. Aim at something! As James Allen quips, everyone should "conceive of a legitimate purpose" in his or her heart. For now, aim at something, however base it may be. On your journey forward, God will continue to elevate your aim, from animalistic self-serving desires to an others-focused mentality. In following Him, we transition from building our own kingdoms to seeking His wonderful Kingdom.

If you don't feel that you are embarking on a great purpose, or still feel lost as to what that purpose may be, you are not alone. For now, set your sights on the masterful performance of your current task, no matter how insignificant it may seem to you. Be fully present where you are until it is time for a change. Bloom where you are planted and soon you may have opportunities to flourish in different soil or you will find beauty right where you are through a shift in your perspective.

> *"There are two great days in a person's life – the day we are born and the day we discover why." ~ William Barclay*

REFLECTION:

It's time to explore why you're on this planet. Spend some quiet time reflecting on your purpose. Then write out and complete this sentence on a blank sheet:

"The reason I exist is to..."

A helpful tip is to keep on writing thoughts to complete this statement until one brings you to tears or fills you with a surge of energy. For some, you'll have tapped into your deeper knowing when it starts connecting with your emotions.

Don't worry about perfecting your purpose statement the first time. Write something! Then adjust as you evolve.

"You can't edit a blank page." ~ *Jodi Picoult*

CHAPTER 8

How to Make it Count

My anxiety attacks were getting progressively worse as the days went on. By the spring of that year, I was suffering from frequent sleepless nights, my head felt like it was spinning and I struggled to think clearly. I had almost zero motivation to do anything productive. I brought my struggles to a friend of mine named Jonathan, because I know that our struggles have more power over us the longer we keep them hidden in the dark. Through our conversation, I found out that he had been facing the same set of symptoms a few years prior. In the parking lot, sitting in his car in front of the gym where he exercises, he had a major epiphany. He realized that the root of his anxiety stemmed from a severe lack of vision and purpose in his life.

> *"Without vision people perish."* ~ *Proverbs 29:18*

His story resonated deeply and I knew I was facing a similar situation. After talking to Jonathan, I realized that I had to search below the surface of my emotions to see what was underneath. Anxiety, like other adverse mental conditions, can be a helpful symptom. Just as a cough is a symptom which indicates there is something going on in your body below the surface, anxiety, depression, and the like are symptoms which indicate that there is inner space to uncover for us to live more fully. In a way, pain, whether mental, physical, or even spiritual, is a beautiful thing. Pain lets us know something is wrong and gives us an opportunity to make changes before we end up with serious illnesses or debilitating injuries. While most people loathe the presence of pain, I have learned to welcome pain as a cherished friend, truly one of the few friends who loves me enough to be brutally honest with me at all times.

Here is what I discovered. I had been letting other people dictate the direction of my life rather than prayerfully setting the course and steering my own ship in submission to God's direction. I was living in response to what everyone else needed – or wanted – me to be and do. My life was mostly reactive instead of proactive. I was simply responding to opportunities as they arose with no real measuring tool that helped me filter out the good opportunities from the bad ones. I was burned out and disillusioned by my own folly.

So I followed what Jonathan did to help get him out of his own rut. Instead of going into the gym that day, Jonathan found a quiet place and mapped out his major goals for each five-year increment in his life, writing it all down in his journal. Which major milestones would mark the years from the age of 31-35? And 36-40? And so on and so forth until he reached the age of 120.

I found a good coffee shop, grabbed some sheets of paper, and contemplatively mapped out my life in five-year chunks, highlighting the major accomplishments that would mark that period of time. This activity was helpful for me, not because it was the definitive roadmap for my life but because I had put my dreams on paper with reasonable timelines.

Of course, we pursue our goals with passion all while holding them loosely. God's plans for our lives are much better than our plans. A good friend of mine appropriately calls life "the divine improv" as a reminder of the way we are to approach the present moment with an adaptive attitude. We find freedom and a much larger destiny when we hold our dreams with open hands. This way, God can take from us the lesser and give the greater as He pleases.

Writing out my goals in this manner was a good step in the right direction, but it wasn't quite enough to scratch the deeper itch for true meaning. All I came up with was more of 'what' I wanted to do, but these activities did nothing to help chart my overall course. Seeing what I wrote gave me some clues as to what was important to me at the time and what my priorities were, but there was definitely more to uncover. As it turned out, some of what I was already doing fit well within my short- and long-term goals, but I really needed to know whether or not the goals I was setting and the actions I was taking contributed positively to my overall purpose and legacy at all.

A conversation with one of my fathers, Keith, has stuck with me to this day. He is a beautiful soul who has experienced a lot in life. Prior to his radical life transformation in following Jesus, and later marrying my mom, he had been married three times and led what he would call a "wild life". In our chat, he shared that he had not really started following The Path until he was in his forties, and he still faces tremendous pain and regret from the choices he made in his younger years. With tears in his eyes, he said, "Justin, you're walking on the narrow path at a much younger age than I did. You need to realize that you have an incredible opportunity. If you will stay on the path, you have the opportunity to live an entire life that counts."

Wow. What would it look like to live an entire life that "counts" towards something more meaningful than my own ego? What would happen if I truly lived from my authentic soul during my time here on this earth? Forgetting the fear of what would happen if things went wrong while I followed my path, I started getting a glimpse of what could go right if I followed my path.

No matter how young or old you are now, you have the opportunity to live the rest of your life on purpose. You can't change the past, but the exciting news is that your future has yet to be written and you hold the pen. And since the future is written by our actions in the present, it's crucial that we line up our current movements with where we really want to go. Otherwise, we can easily end up a long way from where we wanted to be.

Several years ago, I made a big mistake during a dialogue with an acquaintance. I accidentally provoked a monster and I wasn't expecting it at all. All I did was ask him a simple question: "Who did you really want to be when you were younger?" At the time, my friend had a good-paying job as a manager working in a company that sold construction materials. "Don't do that," he said sharply. "Do what?" I asked. "Don't poke at that," he replied. "I put those dreams to sleep a long time ago. It takes a lot of work to numb yourself enough to mindlessly run on the hamster wheel. It's like when you finally get your kid to bed, after a long struggle, and then someone comes barging in his room and wakes him up."

And this is how most of us live. We spend our energy putting our dreams to sleep and numb ourselves through various forms of self-repression. The danger of this lifestyle is that we risk only existing, and never truly living.

I'm not knocking his occupation at all. It was a good job that supported him and his family. But what upset me is the fact that he didn't end up there on purpose; he ended up there by default. And from there, instead of finding some purpose in his current work, which is possible, he just clocked in on Monday and spent his week trying to get to the weekend. He didn't care about what he was doing. His heart and soul weren't in his work at all. So what's the alternative?

When taking a journey anywhere, the first thing we need to determine is our destination. Only then can we begin to analyze the different paths that could get us there.

We have to begin with the end in mind.

In my consulting work, I like to lead my clients through an activity I call the "Legacy Map". In this activity, we seek, together, to extract the deep purpose of their souls and discover practical steps needed to actually achieve their worthwhile goals. By the time we complete the activity, my clients and I have developed a workable 'roadmap' to help them get from where they currently are to where they want to be, and more importantly, to help them walk powerfully towards *who* they want to be. To do this, we start with the end.

We start the activity by exploring the end destination with probing questions like: "How do you want to be remembered at the end of this lifetime? What major goals would you like to accomplish

over your lifetime? What type of legacy do you want to leave behind?"

Once we've established the destination, we work backwards to chart the course towards their legacy and look at the immediate steps they can take to move forward in the direction of their dreams. In doing this exercise, I love seeing the lightbulb moment when the person comes to the realization that their purpose is actually within reach. That never gets old for me.

When embarking on a journey of any kind, we first need to nail down the most crucial piece of information: Where are we going? We have to set the destination first. From there, we can analyze the many ways we could get there and decide on a path. But without a destination, we have no way of knowing whether or not we're getting any closer to where we are supposed to be. And the result is that usually, we end up somewhere completely random instead of where we really wanted to be.

We should have a clear picture of what it looks like to 'arrive'. If you're traveling to Toronto, there are clues to let you know you've made it. You'll see the CN Tower. You'll see the stadium where the Blue Jays baseball team plays. You'll see a beautiful array of people from all different cultures. These are some markers to let you know you've reached the city of Toronto. It's important that we know our destination and gain an understanding of what it would look like to land there.

A common mistake people make, because it seems more logical, is that they simply run their race facing forward from the very beginning. Let's consider a 100-metre dash race to help us understand why this is a problem. Most of us would start the 100-metre dash by lining up at the starting line. That sounds normal, right? We get on our mark, we get set, and then we go. We run as hard as we possibly can and hope that we somehow manage to get a decent result.

Here is the alternative that makes the difference between good and great; it is how the professionals run their races. Instead of simply lining up and running the race forward, the pros walk all the way to the finish line long before the race even begins. They see the end goal and understand what it would look like to finish the race. They visualize themselves running well. Then, beginning from the finish line, they work their way backwards, figuring out the pace they should run, the types of strides they would have to take to reach the finish line, and the training they need to undertake to achieve their best result. They begin with the end in mind.

I like to revisit the "Legacy Map" activity for myself every three months to track my progress and to recalibrate my goals. Over time, certain goals become less important to me while others rise as higher priorities. Along the path, I also discover new goals that I never would've imagined before. The further we travel, the more our field of vision expands as we discover greater passions, dreams, and opportunities along the way.

PRINCIPLE #8: PLAN BACKWARDS

In vision setting and goal planning, it is critical for us to aim at the right things and to measure what matters. Western culture is far too driven by money and status, but these aren't what matter most. No one on their deathbed asks for someone to bring them their shiny car.

I think of death often. Some of my friends think this is morbid, but I find it helpful. It's not that I want to die. It's that I ponder what the end of my life will look like and what types of things I'd want people to say about me after I'm gone, realizing that for all of us our time here on earth is short no matter how many years we live.

Facing our own mortality, as some people are forced to do through the diagnosis of a terminal illness or a close call with death, has a way of naturally reorganizing our priorities. We would do well to consider the fleeting nature of life often. In this light, we realize that the outcomes of our lives are better measured by how we lived, how we loved, whom we were able to help, and other meaningful targets, instead of focusing on what the world glorifies as significant. Looking at life from the eternal viewpoint can give us a much more accurate perspective on our current realities.

Contemplating the bigger picture helps us set targets that matter. For example, when setting the strategy for our company, Good Coffee, we set 'giving goals' instead of 'getting goals.' We first looked at how much money we wanted to reinvest into the coffee growing communities through empowering projects, and how we wanted to make a difference in the lives of everyone involved, from the farmers to our customers. From there, we charted out how much revenue it would take for us to accomplish these worthwhile goals, and we worked out our sales targets correspondingly. We started with setting our sights on what mattered, then worked backwards towards the practical steps of how to get there.

Good Coffee is about transforming lives through coffee and doing it in a way where all of the people in the supply chain, and the earth, are cared for in the process. Coffee is the vehicle that allows us to move forward and revenue is the fuel that keeps the vehicle running. But money is not the point.

Revenue is the result of adding value to peoples' lives. Profitability is the result of adding value to peoples' lives in a way that is sustainable long-term. And true wealth in business is the result of adding value to peoples' lives in a way that is sustainable long-term *and* makes sure that the planet and every human involved is thriving. As it turns out in business, we most often erroneously focus on pursuing the effect, rather than putting our energy into the cause. The purpose of a business has to be much bigger than mere profit-chasing for the business to make the world a better place at all. Taking shortcuts, exploiting people, and the like, can get some short-term results but it always comes at a much greater cost.

> *"What good will it be for someone to gain the whole world, yet forfeit their soul?"* ~ *Jesus*

I believe we are heading towards a new era of business that more accurately reflects God's heart for humanity. Within my lifetime, I believe that I will get to experience a period in history where it is no longer profitable for businesses to operate unethically, simply because customers have discovered and activated the tremendous power they have in directing their dollar to the right places. Every dollar we spend is a vote for the type of world we want to live in.

On the quest to live well, we hear a lot about what *not* to do. For example, we know that it's destructive to watch porn. People tell you that you shouldn't watch porn. It's bad for you. It's bad for the many people exploited by the sex industry. It's bad for your relationships. It's bad for your mental health. It fuels human trafficking. Bad. Bad. Bad. And all of that is true to an extent, but knowing what not to do does little to actually change our behavior. Negative emotion is a poor tool when seeking a healthy transformation. Real progress comes when we find an alternative in the opposite direction.

If you were riding a bike, it would be like someone screaming at you, repeatedly, "Don't hit the tree! Don't hit the tree!" Well, guess what? Hearing those words makes you far more likely to hit the tree. Why? Because now you're focused on the tree. And your momentum takes you in the direction of your focus. You go where your eyes are looking.

Instead of the "don't hit the tree" mentality, I propose that you rather exert yourself towards what you *do* want to hit.

Take the aforementioned issue of pornography, as our example. What if men focused on empowering women and finding ways to selflessly serve them, instead of just trying our best *not* to exploit them? Spending energy as a defender, builder, and giver automatically precludes us from being an exploiter, destroyer, or taker. Most people get stuck in the cycle of guilt based on the idea that porn is bad. But telling ourselves that something is "bad" isn't enough for us to change our ways. Rather, there's naturally no energy left for the bad if we've already spent all the energy on the good. What if we became consumed with the magnificence of loving others well, rather than just doing our best not to hurt people?

> *"The secret of change is to focus all of your energy not on fighting the old, but on building the new."* ~ *Socrates*

Evaluate your actions in light of who you want to be. Think, "If I do this, does it get me closer to or further from the person I want to be?" This is a simple measurement tool to help keep you on track. This question can also serve as the first filter when examining a new opportunity. An opportunity has to pass the legacy test. "Does this align with who I am?" From there, you can look deeper and analyze the possibilities further. But it has to line up, from a values standpoint, with who you want to be.

REFLECTION:

Which of my daily actions are taking me further down the right path?
And which actions are steps further from where I want to be?

"Give careful thought to your ways..." ~ *Hosea 1:5*

CHAPTER 9

How to Be a Better Drug Dealer

At the age of fifteen, I began a promising career as a small town drug dealer, supplying high-quality weed to happy customers. It turned out that I was pretty good at it. I sourced out a solid supplier, bought the materials at a wholesale price, organized a paid team of distributors who would deliver the products so that I minimized my own risk, and did the basic accounting to make sure we were turning a profit. It didn't last for very long, but it was a great little business.

When I had my radical encounter with Jesus at the age of seventeen, a lot changed for me. Faced with His holiness and perfection, I began seeing just how ugly my sinful nature was compared to His beauty. In His presence, I was safe and loved but the condition of my heart, the ego, was exposed under the purity and light emanating from the Master.

I was ashamed to look at my past, especially the past few years. I had led so many of my friends astray and I had caused a tremendous amount of pain in the lives of people I cared about. The worst part was, I couldn't hide from this reality. I'm a leader regardless of which direction I'm going. And at this time I was leading people towards terrible destinations. I was using my God-given talents for the dark side. In my mind, I had determined that the real problem wasn't just that I was doing bad things. To me, the problem was that I *was* bad. I was irredeemably rotten all the way at the core. I thought I had to get rid of everything I was in order to live a life that would please God, but that's not true at all.

Spending more time with Jesus over the following years, He revealed a much deeper truth to my soul. My gifts are my gifts, no matter how I choose to use them. God doesn't take the gifts away. That's scary because we can easily misuse what God has given us; an obvious and extreme example would be to look at the tremendous talent and charisma of Hitler.

Or take human sexuality as another poignant example. Sex is a magical gift created by God. Engaged the right way, it leads to deep connection and intimacy. Engaged the wrong way it leads to the use of another person, unhealthy emotional ties between people, or can even do much worse damage, as in situations like rape or sex trafficking.

When we walk in sin, missing the mark, these distorted versions of our talents create natural consequences. I'm convinced that God doesn't go out of His way to punish us when we sin. It's rather that He allows sin to have its way. There are natural consequences to living contrary to God's way. Yes, He disciplines us out of love when we're getting off track like a good parent would, because He knows that what we're doing is harmful and He hates to see us harming ourselves or others, but He doesn't punish us in the way we think of punishment. Sin does a good enough job of that all by itself.

Engaging with Jesus helped me realized that my drug dealing was simply a twisted version of a beautiful gift. I was living a corrupted and perverted version of who I was meant to be. On its own, the gift was healthy, but I had twisted it. Fundamentally I was created good, but through the unchecked ego, my gifts took on their inherent path of destruction. It wasn't that I was forever doomed to hurt people as a drug dealer; I just had the gift entrepreneurship. I had been using this talent to do some awful things, but it didn't have to be this way. I didn't have to throw away who I was to walk the narrow path. I had to give who I was to Jesus, so that He could redeem and baptize me to be employed for His higher purposes.

When I had this epiphany, I started seeing clues pointing to the pattern of entrepreneurship from way back in my childhood. I was the kid who ran a lemonade stand on the block. I collected bugs from my garden, organized a bug zoo, and charged other kids 25 cents to come to see it. I think the bug zoo only had 5 total clients, but not every business idea takes off, I guess. The list went on. I was an entrepreneur.

Many years after this realization, I went on to start our coffee company, Good Coffee. It was about two years into running the business when I put more of the pieces together. Caffeine is technically considered a drug. It's a stimulant. So now, by selling coffee, I'm a drug dealer for Jesus. I'm a gospel gangster. By the grace of God, I get to use my gifts in a way that adds value and gives dignity to thousands of people around the world. That's awesome.

One time I found myself in another "existential crisis" type of conversation with a good friend of mine. She, in tears, was struggling to find her calling and purpose in life. I suggested that we could start by looking at her gifts and talents to find some clues. Uh oh, I guess I shouldn't have gone there. That led to more tears as she exclaimed, "I don't think I have any gifts at all!" As far as she was concerned, there was nothing special about her. There was nothing of value she could offer the world.

The week before this conversation, she ran a weekend camp for kids at her church. She planned the theme, organized the entire event, and recruited and coordinated all of the volunteers. The weekend went amazingly. She received great reviews and feedback from the kids who attended and their parents. She told me all of this at the start of our conversation as we were catching up on life before things got emotional in discussing her purpose. So I brought it up again.

"What about the camp you just organized?" I asked.

"What does that have to do with discovering my gifts?!" she replied sharply, "that camp was easy to pull off. Anyone could do that!"

"Um… no, actually…" I replied. "Not everyone could do that. For me, a notoriously unorganized person, that event would take astronomically more energy and effort to achieve results even close to as good as what you just executed. I would need a bunch more people around me, including someone like you as the main organizer, for it to be well-run and successful. The fact that it was easy for you to organize that is precisely what *makes* it a gift."

PRINCIPLE #9: CELEBRATE YOUR AWESOMENESS

We often dismiss our gifts even when they are right in front of our faces. When something comes naturally to us, we tend to take it for granted. We don't think of that thing as special, so we discount it as something that we think anyone could do. But not everyone could do that. In fact, no one else on the planet could do it like you do. Our gifts flow from our areas of grace, from the areas of our lives that come easily and smoothly to us. When we focus energy on further developing our natural areas of grace, that's when we can discover the virtuosos hidden within us all.

Which of your gifts have you dismissed?

For example, maybe saying nice things to people comes naturally to you so you think it's too easy and that it doesn't count as a gift. Wrong! That would be called the 'gift of encouragement.' It really is not easy for most humans to find something uplifting to say about someone else. A good way to discover your gifts is to ask people who know you what things they see you doing well, or what types of character traits they like about you. You may learn that these people see more in you than you see in yourself. And once we find our gifts, we should look for ways to use them towards serving others.

> *"The meaning of life is to find your gift. The purpose of life is to give it away."* ~ Pablo Picasso

I love the story of David and Goliath for many reasons, but recently a few pieces of the story grabbed my attention in a brand new way.

As the quick version of the story goes, a young shepherd is asked by his father to bring his older brothers provisions, as his brothers served at the front line of the army in Israel's battle against the Philistines. When he gets there, he sees this towering giant of a man from the Philistine army come down and shout obscenities at the Israelites. Knowing how powerful God is, David volunteers to go and fight him. His brothers make fun of him, basically telling him to stay in his lane. David decides to go anyway. Then Saul, the King of Israel at the time, says that if David really wanted to take on the battle, he would help him. Saul volunteers his own royal armor. David tries it on and finds it too clunky. From there, he finds rocks from a nearby river and grabs the sling that he had been using as a shepherd to protect his sheep from predators, goes down into the valley, and kills the giant.

There's a lot to unpack in this story, but I want to focus on three things that impacted me:

1) We need to dismiss haters.

David's brothers ridiculed him for even thinking about taking on this enormous task. To them, he was nothing more than the youngest brother, charged to keep watch over the family's smelly sheep. David had to consciously decide to put their negative comments and his own self-doubts aside to proceed with his mission. He did not let the glaring discouragement from some of the people closest to him dissuade him. We, too, need to press through discouragement into the courage available to us when we walk our paths.

Note that a 'hater' is *not* necessarily anyone and everyone who disagrees with me. Some people are just genuinely concerned for our well-being and may be able to see the situation more clearly than we do. We would do well to listen and sift through what we can learn from the conversation. It's like panning for gold. We shake out the dirt and take what is helpful.

Instead, a 'hater' is someone who, because of their own insecurities and small-mindedness, doesn't really want to see you succeed. Or they make discouraging comments without knowing who you are or what you're actually capable of. We cannot afford for these opinions to hold us back.

2) We need to use who we are.

King Saul offered David some incredible armor, but it didn't fit properly. It was clunky. David chose to use the tools that he knew how to use. Instead of trying to be somebody he wasn't, he took on the challenge at hand using the skills he had acquired during his time in the wilderness with the sheep.

Sometimes, the structures and tools that work for someone else just don't fit us. There's nothing wrong with that. It's easy to find ourselves trying to be someone we're not, especially when the armor looks so good on the other person. We need to stop this vanity. With God, we have what it takes to conquer the seemingly impossible tasks that He has allowed on our paths. It's time to use who we are to make a difference in the world. Understand that it won't look like anyone else's life. We weren't created to fit in. We were created to stand out. Be who you are.

3) We're better equipped than we think.

Most people would feel ill-prepared facing a giant with only a sling and some rocks. But for David, his wealth experience using this powerful long-range weapon gave him a distinct advantage over the immobile mass of a human opposing him.[7] David wasn't *just* a shepherd. He *was* a shepherd. It was precisely his odd and unsightly occupation that gave him an unexpected benefit in this battle. We truly have no idea how God will eventually use our wiring and our experiences to catapult us into areas of our destinies that we would never have dreamed of.

Furthermore, after David knocked out Goliath using a sling and a stone, he ran over to the giant and used Goliath's own sword to finish the job. In one sense then, David might not have had everything he needed to defeat this giant when the battle first began. It seems that he only had what he needed to start the process. The rest of what he needed came later.

God further equips us along the journey with the additional tools, resources, and people needed to complete the mission. The point is to start walking and use what we currently have at our disposal.

---

[7] Again, I am indebted to Malcolm Gladwell for his fresh perspective on the David and Goliath story in his book "David and Goliath".

REFLECTION:

Which of my awesome gifts do I underutilize or undervalue?

CHAPTER 10

How to Actually Get Somewhere

We began Good Coffee with severe gaps in a few crucial areas of business. To set the stage, here's a complete list of what we had at our disposal:

- Passion.
- An idea.
- The grace of God.
- That's about it.

Here's what we were missing:

- Business experience.
- Any dollars, of our own, at all.
- Expertise in the areas of marketing, finance, operations (or anything else that matters in business).
- Coffee sourcing knowledge.
- Coffee roasting knowledge.

- Really any coffee knowledge (other than the fact that we liked to drink coffee).
- Familiarity with the distribution of consumable products.
- Supply-chain management skills.
- I could go on… but you get the point.

It turns out that getting started is not easy, but it is very simple. Here's the secret:

To begin, begin.

The only way Good Coffee materialized is because at some point we just started walking, and along the way, we got help from people who had walked similar paths before us. We simply began moving, taking active and tangible steps in the direction of our dreams. From there, God started providing everything we needed to progress. We found investors who were willing to take a chance on our idea. We met people, always providentially, who had expertise in the areas where we were lacking. We found like-hearted allies who believed in the opportunity of making the world a better place through coffee. We leapt and the net appeared. Beyond all this, we learned exponentially more about business and life through experience than we could have in a classroom setting. Book knowledge is a great supplement that can serve to further equip you with different tools, but there is no teacher that can replace the simple act of doing.

> *"The journey of a thousand miles begins with one step."*
>
> *~ Lao Tzu*

If you wait until you *feel* ready to start, you never will. There will always be more knowledge to acquire, more stars you'd like to see align, more life stability desired. There comes a point, however, when you know that the time for action has come and you mustn't delay walking through that door any longer. The truth is, you're not ready for what's on the other side, but you will have everything you need to overcome each new obstacle as each one arises. Therein lies the beauty of embarking on the adventure.

If the dream doesn't scare you, the dream isn't big enough. If you can confidently accomplish the goal on your own, the goal is too small. We must dream dreams so big that they would be completely doomed to fail without the presence of God and the help of others. Striving on your own you absolutely *do not* have what it takes, and that is the most freeing and incredible news.

Our emotions are extremely poor indicators when measuring the validity of an undertaking. Either over-excitement or excessive fear can prove deadly. Simply saying "yes" to a good-looking path out of excitement can take you to places you'd never have wished to end up. Conversely, avoiding a worthwhile path out of fear can cause you to miss out on the most beautiful destinations.

Instead, follow the path of peace. True peace, the kind that God gives us, is the only sure compass on the path to fulfillment. Peace is the God-given stillness in the soul that disregards any physiological or emotional response. This same peace breeds deep conviction, which provides stability for your soul through the inevitable storms along the way.

Even when examined from a physiological standpoint, it turns out that we really cannot afford to wait until we *feel* motivated. Your brain's chief responsibility is to ensure your survival. Simply, your brain is designed to keep you alive. To do so, it seeks to avoid any and all risk. At the sight of something that looks dangerous, the brain begins to fire distress signals, releasing hormones designed to stimulate a fear response and cause the feeling of anxiety. The only way to venture outside of our comfort zones, outside of survival-mode, and to get to the amazing places we are afraid to go is to override the natural fear signals of our brains and *choose* to move forward.

Interestingly, an exhilarating rush of adrenaline, another physiological response from the brain, waits for us right on the other side of our fear. When you finally take the leap and jump out of an airplane to skydive, for example, you experience an overwhelming sensation of ecstasy. Up until that point, you had been spending your time and energy fearing what might be.

Here's what I mean by that. If you go skydiving, you will experience far more fear on the night before than when you're in mid-air falling rapidly towards the ground. While lying in your bed, though completely safe and warm, you'll project irrational fear by anticipating what is to come. You will then feel an escalating fear the rest of the way, most intensely while standing with your toes over the edge of the plane's open door. Again, this fear is completely irrational and anticipatory because technically, here in the plane, you are still extremely safe. At the height of the real danger, however, while you are free-falling at intense speeds towards the earth, you have access to a feeling of complete abandon and freedom. It is in the anticipation of danger, while logically at the lowest levels of actual danger, that we find the greatest sense of fear. At the peak of real danger, however, we manage to find moments of true bliss once we've taken the leap.

The rewards of progress come almost exclusively by acts of the will that result in action. We rarely, if ever, execute difficult, worthwhile endeavors because we *felt* like taking chances. Even if we happen to step out boldly towards our destinies in emotionally-charged moments of courage, we still cannot rely on our fleeting and faltering feelings to carry us through the unavoidable days where, void of all positive emotion, the only things moving us forward are the raw decisions of the will to take one more reluctant step in the right direction at a time.

@kardiagallery

130

PRINCIPLE #10: GET MOVING NOW.
YOUR FEELINGS WILL CATCH UP

I think God tricks us into getting married.

Marriage is the most beautiful God-ordained institution on the planet that I know of. The deep covenantal marriage relationship is the closest earthly image we have to God's ideal relationship with humans. It's a glimpse into His relentless, sacrificial pursuit of that relationship. As we see by looking at Jesus' stories, He often uses a wedding or marriage parable to get His point across. Marriage is amazing. Simultaneously, marriage done well is also the most challenging undertaking on the entire planet.

The call of marriage is to intentionally serve the other, laying down your life to put your partner's needs ahead of your own. And that requires God - because it is completely unnatural. Love has to be super-natural because our natural, primal default is towards selfishness. The animal instinct in us lends towards self-preservation. Furthermore, having someone in your life who knows you intimately and completely – at your best and at your worst – continually exposes the filthy mess inside your heart and brings the gravity of your egocentric nature to the light. Had anyone known how completely (though wonderfully and constructively) marriage would destroy him or her, few would venture to undertake this type of covenantal relationship. Many are disappointed by marriage simply because they have utterly confused its purpose in their own minds.

If we view marriage primarily as a means to happiness and the fulfillment of our own desires, we are in for a rude awakening. This couldn't be further from its purpose. The purpose of marriage is not to create happiness for us. Its purpose is to forge holiness in us. Its purpose is to push us towards growth. How unpleasant this feels depends largely on how stubbornly we resist, or how readily we submit to, change. Marriage serves to make us better, to evolve us, if we let it, into higher versions of ourselves. Happiness and deep joy are some of the delicious fruits, the by-products of a healthy marriage, but we become extremely disappointed if we hold the expectation that such the union exists for our own pleasure. That said, the euphoria of truly knowing, and being known by, another person in covenantal marriage, along with the soul expansion that results from this exchange, completely eclipses all of the agony that accompanies growth.

I say this because in some ways, too, I feel as though God tricked me into starting Good Coffee. The process of entrepreneurship, though delightfully transformative to my character, has been almost unbearably painful at times in the way it exposes the shadowy iniquities in the recesses of my heart. Like a good marriage, walking your path isn't always easy, but it is worth it.

I'm not convinced that the operational procedure of "Ready. Aim. Fire." actually applies to real life. The more I see and hear through my own experience and through learning from the journeys of others, it seems more accurately to be "Aim. Fire. Ready." We should definitely set our aim before we let the arrows fly or we will end up off the mark, but we cannot afford to wait until we feel *ready,* or we will keep coming up with excuses not to shoot at all. I'm convinced that God uses the journey itself to make us ready along the way.

If something is really important to you, you'll find a way. If it's not important enough to you, you'll find an excuse.

> *"He who watches the wind will never sow, and he who watches the clouds will never reap." ~ Ecclesiastes 11:4*

It will never feel like the right time for you to get going. Get over your fixation on making sure the conditions are perfect. If you're obsessed with watching the weather of your life's seasons, watching the markets, waiting to see what North Korea will do, waiting for the idyllic moment, you'll never get your boots on the ground or your hands dirty. You can't possibly get a harvest if you don't put any seeds in the ground. There's just no way around that.

I'm not advocating for an irresponsible or flippant approach to life where we just start things at random. As we saw in the chapter on *How to Make it Count*, effective planning is a major key to reaching your goals. I am saying, though, that many dreams die from the paralysis of analysis. Many of us suffocate our dreams through over-thinking and self-doubting, masked by false-righteousness and disguised as prudence. Maybe you are not being prudent. Perhaps you are living afraid.

Some people, fully deceived, even go so far as to defer the responsibility for their cowardice and inaction onto God saying, "I'm waiting on the Lord…" Waiting on the Lord is most often an *active* waiting. If you are waiting for someone to come over to your house, you prepare your house for his or her arrival. That's what true waiting looks like. If the Lord has spoken clearly, "don't move until I say so" then, of course, we ought to obey His instruction. More often though, I believe people use the phrase "waiting on the Lord" to justify the cowardly delay of the missions they are supposed to embark upon and make their timidity sound noble and magnanimous. If you are truly waiting on the Lord, that is a good thing. If you are hesitating out of fear, that is not good.

You've likely heard of the 5 P's: "Proper Preparation Prevents Poor Performance" and that's true. As Abraham Lincoln famously said, "Give me six hours to chop down a tree and I will spend the first four sharpening the axe." We must prepare well. But many of us use overextend 'preparation phases' as excuses to remain stagnant and frozen. In fact, you are not sharpening the axe. You're just thinking about sharpening the axe and all of the things that could go wrong once you start cutting down the tree. And you're stuck. At some point, you have to just start chopping down the tree.

If you're in the perpetual cycle of product development, then hurry up and get moving! Get your product to market. Test it in the real world. Refine it. Test it again. Adjust your strategy. Test it again. Fail quickly so that you can find out what actually works. But please move past incessantly tweaking the product behind closed doors with no real-world feedback mechanisms. Perfection isn't the goal. Progress is the goal.

> *"Art is never finished, only abandoned."* ~ *Leonardo da Vinci*

Plan your work. Then work your plan. We get in big trouble when we do just one or the other. Some people start going without a plan at all (this would be my default if I was left to my own devices) and spend a lot of time spinning their tires. Others plan forever and go nowhere. They're all talk.

With that said, I am convinced that action beats inaction. When a ship is sitting in harbor it takes a whole bunch of strong people using chains to turn its direction even slightly, or it takes another ship already in motion to pull it and redirect it. When a ship is at sea, however, it only takes a small rudder to change its course. It is much easier to direct a ship that is already in motion. In the same way, it is much easier for God to redirect you and help you get on the right course when your life is in motion. Trust that He is big enough to get you on course and keep you on course. Get out there.

As my friend Ryan reminded me during a recent meeting:

"Set the goal. Set the plan.

Then, forget the goal. And work the plan."

It is also important to note that, while it is true that God "has given you everything you need for life and godliness", most of us erroneously take this statement to mean that now we don't need Him or anyone else. What God has

135

placed in your heart is much too much for you to accomplish on your own. It requires His grace and it requires help from other people. He did it that way on purpose. "Everything you need" happens to include a lot more than what you have all by yourself. The idea of being 'self-made' is a complete myth and a worthless pursuit. Pursuing the self-made, lone wolf lifestyle leads only to destruction, mostly the destruction of healthy relationships. Don't try to walk this alone.

Here's one of the craziest things for me to wrap my mind around: I'm an author now! I really do hope one of my high school English teachers, who had to kick me out of class for being disruptive, gets to read one of my books at some point. When I realized that I might be able to add value to someone's life by sharing what I've learned along my journey, I added: "become an author" to my written list of goals. Now I'm an author. That's wild.

The point worth noting is that I'm not an author because I'm necessarily good at writing. I'm an author because I wrote. It's that simple. I just finally managed to sit down long enough to do the work. I ended up enlisting Trevor Lund as my writing coach because I didn't have the discipline to go through the steps by myself, and I knew in my soul that it was important for this book to be written. If you're repeatedly struggling to achieve a worthwhile goal, it might be time to get a coach in that area. Accountability does wonders.

Now get moving. Remember, nothing works unless you do. Talk is cheap.

Find a need then fill a need. When it comes to a business idea, we would do well to think in terms of adding value to others. What problems are we solving for people? How are we improving on something? How are we serving humanity? Once we've found ways to make others' lives better, it's time to get started.

> *"The best time to plant a tree was 20 years ago.*
> *The second best time is today."*
> ~ *Chinese Proverb*

REFLECTION:

What would be the courageous step for me to take right now?

CHAPTER 11

How to Tell the Time

Ok, you're ready to get started and go all-in! Ah, but not so fast, my friend.

You may have heard the story of General Cortez. As legend has it, he and his army landed on the shores in a foreign land that they wished to conquer. The problem was, they were terribly outnumbered by the opposition. In the middle of the night, he secretly commanded his generals to go burn all of the boats that they arrived in. With the boats on fire in the background – an epic scene to be sure – he said some courageous words like, "The only way for us to see our loved ones and our homes again is to leave here in their ships." Then this outnumbered, now highly inspired and motivated group of warriors won the battle. This is how we should live our lives all the time, right? We should do away with our safety nets and throw away our Plan Bs because they only get in the way of our Plan As! Or should we?

The answer is: sometimes. There is a word of caution for stories like this. We hear them and we take them to be a one-size-fits-all formula for success. "Burning the boats" is a strategy. It is not the only way to win a battle. This strategy could work brilliantly under very specific conditions, like when you find yourself with your back against the wall and you are at a severe disadvantage with little at your disposal in terms of leverage.

Sometimes we need to go all-in, throw caution to the wind, and create "win or die" scenarios for us to work out of. The right kind of pressure facilitates tremendous results for some. Forced to find ways out, we discover that necessity is the mother of all invention and we create beauty, which we could not have otherwise realized. Other times, though, this approach destroys everything. This strategy is only useful some of the time.

As the entrepreneurship lifestyle is dear to my heart, I am increasingly concerned about my fellow dreamers and doers. Research suggests that at least 30% of entrepreneurs actively suffer from depression.[8] What's more alarming is the fact that depression is a leading indicator of suicide. It is possible for us to crack under the weight of our endeavors – with businesses to run, teams to manage, bills to pay, families to feed and employees' livelihoods (along with those of their families) all under our responsibility – it is a lot for us humans to carry on our shoulders and most people improperly try to carry the burden alone. The word depression is well constructed because I can testify from experience that it really feels like you're being "pressed down" (or de-pressed) under the weight of the stressors. We must find healthy ways to relieve this burden.

If you are an entrepreneur, or if you happen to find yourself under toxic amounts of stress for other reasons, please let people know how you're actually doing. "I'm fine" or "I'll be fine" isn't going to cut it. There's a ton of pressure for us to look like we have

---

[8] Dr. Michael Freeman, University of California, San Francisco. That number is likely much higher because of unreported cases due to the stigma around depression.

our lives together, and that prevents many of us from talking about our mental health. Stop pretending and get help. Don't wait until your ship has almost sunk before you reach out. Treat mental health like you would treat the flu. Go see the doctor when you have symptoms, long before you are at the point when you cannot even manage to get up. Consistent feelings of anxiety, deep apathy, or stress are symptoms of deeper issues. Talk to someone you trust.

If you know an entrepreneur, there may be better questions you could ask her or him. If you have a good relationship with the person, the deeper questions like, "Has the new venture contributed additional strain on your relationships?" or "What are you doing to manage your stress during the intense start-up phase?" are far more helpful than the usually disingenuous, "How's business?"

On the entrepreneurial journey, there are instances where going 'all-in' could be precisely the problem causing you to live under too much pressure. It's because here, there is no cushion at all. There is no safety net, nothing to fall back on. There is no release valve to lessen the pressure of creating meaning in the world. Some people resort to false means of creating what feels like a temporary relief. They start doing cocaine, they have affairs, or they take their own lives, to name a few examples.

Applying the 'burn the boats' principle, a good and useful idea, at the wrong time got me – and Good Coffee – in a lot of trouble. When Good Coffee started, I was still shackled with a mountain of personal debt in the form of student loans. I had no reserve funds saved as a backup. A year into running the company I got married to the love of my life, which was a major blessing, but it certainly added a healthy amount of financial pressure on to my shoulders. We started the company with $50,000 *under* what we needed as an investment. And somehow under these circumstances, I decided that the best way to grow the company was to 'burn the boats' and go all-in. It was awful.

My family had to face undue financial stress. The company paid me a tiny monthly stipend, which was helpful, except for the fact that the company really couldn't afford to pay me at all. Without operating capital in the bank, those funds really needed to be reinvested in infrastructure and hiring people who were qualified to cover the major gaps in my skill set and wiring. I could not pay my helpful and qualified staff anything, let alone anything close to what their time was worth.

PRINCIPLE #11: KNOW WHAT TIME IT IS

Adam Grant, in his stimulating book *Originals*, dedicates an entire chapter to highlighting a few great companies, like the well-known eyeglass distributor, Warby Parker, who succeeded precisely because they did not 'burn the boats.' Instead, they did the opposite. They purposely kept their safety nets, working on their business as a side-project while working full-time at other jobs until their own company reached a crucial tipping point. They worked until they could afford to hire themselves and spend all of their time focusing on growing the business. In these cases, having a backup option provided these entrepreneurs with the security and confidence to take big, calculated risks in order to grow their business, all while thinking objectively and unemotionally about the company's finances because they were not, at that point, dependent on the company for their entire livelihoods.

One of my mentors uses a concept called the 'leap-number.' This approach may be a practical way to provide a solid safety net for your venture, and reduce (not eliminate) the natural stress of taking on the unknown. A leap-number is an easily measurable, predetermined metric that you submit yourself to in the process of timing the 'all-in' stage of your journey. Most often it's a financial indicator, such as having a certain amount of money saved up. It dictates when you jump. For example, I know of a few people who commit to saving the equivalent of three months' living expenses in a separate account before launching. Others will jump into their businesses with both feet only when the businesses have generated monthly *profits* in excess of their living expenses for three consecutive months.

Having a solid idea of your 'leap number' becomes the compass that allows you to know at what point you are justified in taking the leap of faith. Keep in mind, it is still a big leap no matter when you jump, but having a solid launch-point mitigates risk and stacks the odds further in your favor.

Single people, although most of them erroneously seem to be in a big hurry to end their loneliness and quench their insecurities by finding life-partners, have tremendous opportunities in their singleness to take much crazier risks than others with spouses and piles of kids. If you are currently reading this as a single person, please use this season of life to take wilder, calculated risks. Now is the time. Quit spending your time and energy wishing you were in a relationship as if another person could fulfill you anyway, and start being ridiculously awesome right now.

When it comes to relationships, I've noticed a pattern. It seems to be at precisely the time when you stop *needing* someone to complete you, and you become whole and secure without having to be co-dependent on another person that, ironically, you find yourself healthy enough to be in a relationship. When someone is living fully and doing things that matter, he or she gives off the most wonderfully attractive energy. At that point, God can finally bring that person into your life, because before this you likely would've somehow sabotaged the relationship. His timing is perfect. Then, you will be in a relationship asking, "what can I give?" instead of "what can I get?" The goal is to know and love where you are at in life. Take advantage of where you are rather than always wishing you were somewhere, or someone, else.

"There is a time for everything under the sun."
~ *Ecclesiastes 3:1*

Then what's the right answer? Should you burn the boats? Or should you create a solid safety net before launching out? As my friend Ben often says when faced with a multi-layered question, "It depends". There are situations that would warrant using one of those strategies, or a combination of both, or even another strategy not mentioned here at all. The key to your success is to know what time it is for you.

Spend enough quiet time of reflection, and bounce ideas off of supportive, honest, people in your life, and figure out what season you are in.

If you plant seeds when it is harvest time, no matter how perfectly and diligently you managed to plant the seeds, you simply cannot succeed in your mission to produce a crop. You could have everything else right. You could have great soil, the perfect amount of water and the best agronomist hired to maintain the crop. You could have planted the best seed varietal on the planet, but none of this helps you much if you plant the seeds completely out of season. These seeds, as good as they are in terms of quality, do not stand much of a chance. Success is not merely a matter of doing the right things. We must do the right things at the right times and for the right reasons to achieve worthwhile and lasting results.

Tap into your deeper wisdom, not your emotions. Neither fear nor foolish-optimism should govern your decisions. If you're one who is prone to start things and not finish (like me), it may be wise to slow down, get your life in order, and focus on one undertaking for now, in order to see it through to completion. If you're one who is prone to delay incessantly what you know you should be doing now out of fear, then you should probably stop talking about it and start doing something.

REFLECTION:

What season of life am I in right now?

CHAPTER 12

How to Whole-Ass Something

It's hard for me to focus. My boundless energy and zest for life are undoubtedly God-given assets, yet they can double as my Achilles heel (I did partially rupture my real-life Achilles tendon a few years ago and I don't recommend it – highly overrated). At this very moment, sitting in yet another coffee shop writing this chapter, my mind could wander onto one of the ten fairly important, current tasks yet undone... or I could just spot a shiny object.

Every morning when I wake up, I start the day with approximately seven phenomenal, globe-shaking ideas in my head before my feet even hit the floor. But unfortunately, people don't build a reputation on what they say they're going to do. Our impact depends on actually doing. Lofty speculations, as great as these aims may be, are nothing without action. The true power is found in commitment and relentless execution.

Dreaming is necessary and life-giving. If, however, the vision is not followed by action it will forever remain a fantasy. A dream without a plan and serious action is just a wish. Aim and fire. Don't just aim. And don't just fire. Neither is sufficient on its own. Vision without action is nothing more than a mental exercise. Action without vision is wasted energy.

Once we've got this down, the next key is consistency. Consistency is painfully un-glamorous. And this has been a major area of learning for me over the last couple of years. I'm a fire starter, not always a fire sustainer. It's great to be high-energy, but that energy must be harnessed or else it will be a whirlwind rather than a windmill. I'm still getting there.

> *"Many claim to have unfailing love, but a **faithful** man who can find?"* ~ Proverbs 20:6

Whatever you're doing, be all there. Be completely and fully present. If you're working on multiple projects and the idea of working on just one thing for more than an hour seems as unbearable to you as it does to me, just close all the other windows on your computer and put away the book you were simultaneously reading... then after one focused hour, reward yourself with ten minutes of daydreaming. Do one thing at a time. And do it with all of your might. Sometimes I'll remember something else I had to do. I've learned to just make a note of it (I call this putting the idea in the parking lot) and stay on task. It seems to be enough to scratch the itch. Try it if focus is an issue for you.

@tai.the.girl

I find that I hear from God very clearly before the start of an adventure and it sounds something like this:

"Go this direction and don't get off the path no matter what happens." It's very clear.

Then somewhere on the journey, I start questioning what I heard. I see shiny objects. Or interesting new trails. Or neat opportunities. Some of these things look so good that I really do wonder if my ears were clean when I heard from Him before the journey started. Maybe these are new opportunities from God himself?!

> *"To make even one dream a reality, many other dreams have to be sacrificed on the altar of your imagination."*
> ~ *Erwin McManus*

Why is it so hard to stay the course? I find it a bit funny – and frustrating – because Satan's tactic has been the same from the beginning of time. Often the deception doesn't take a blatant form. In Genesis, all he said to get Adam and Eve off track was something like (I'm paraphrasing here), "Did God *really* say you shouldn't do that? Maybe He doesn't want you to have fun." It was categorically more of a suggestion, just planting a seed of doubt in their hearts. Did He *really* say [insert direction from the Lord], maybe you should [insert an idea that involves us thinking we know better] instead….

Nothing has changed. I find myself doing the right thing, wondering in my mind if it really is the wise thing to do. Something like, "Did God *really* mean it when He said to take a weekly day of Sabbath rest? I could probably achieve more stuff if I just worked all seven days… I'll sleep when I die!" That's stupid. God built me and I'm questioning His plan for how to live the most impactful life. Or,

"I know when I was praying, the Lord spoke strongly to simplify my life and focus on what's important – like my marriage – but there is so much work to be done everywhere else. Maybe I'm missing out on cool stuff." It takes a lot of effort for me to stay on track.

Never forget in the moment of chaos what you determined in the moment of clarity. Even good things can be a distraction. 'Good' can be the biggest threat to 'great'. Trust Him. Stay.

In business, many entrepreneurs fear the niche. Here a lack of focus becomes a subtle, yet effective, slow poison that systematically murders many great ideas and leaves people burned-out. As a dreamer, especially a multi-talented one, the temptation is to try to be all things to all people. Instead, when we try to run the race in this manner, we most often end up being no-thing to no-people. Out of a fear of being pigeonholed, we try to keep our options open and pursue multiple aspects of our vision all at once. We are afraid of finding ourselves in a small niche because the vision we have for the venture is so much bigger than any one area of the business or any single market segment. You want your business to be global in its reach, monumental in its impact, and all-encompassing in its scope.

PRINCIPLE #12: USE A LASER BEAM INSTEAD OF A SHOTGUN

Having a huge, multi-faceted vision is awesome. As mentioned earlier, we know that we can only go as far as we can imagine ourselves going, so we *must* continually expand our vision in order to reach the heights we are destined to reach. The problem is when we try to bite off the entire vision at once. In the marketing world, a good friend of mine and marketing wizard, Taylor Abeel, calls this the 'shotgun approach.' A shotgun fires a whole bunch of little pieces of metal in an outspread fashion, which can work really well at short ranges for specific types of shooting. In business though, we more often need laser-like focus. We do better to channel all of our energy and efforts towards very small niches, master and dominate those small areas, then set our attention on the next pieces of the puzzles. Once we have mastered these areas, then we have permission to expand to other phases of our missions.

Effort and effectiveness are not the same things.

Though I consider the need for war to be obsolete in the current age of civilization, the image of the battle provides helpful illustrations for life and business. Many generals have failed on their missions of trying to take new territories by spreading their troops too thinly from the beginning. In this approach, the general spreads out his troops and sends ships with groups of soldiers to various places along the coast when attempting to gain initial entry to the territory. Like in business, trying to be everywhere at once most usually leads to major losses. To be more effective, a wise general concentrates his entire army in a small, strategic area called the 'beachhead.' Ideally, this unexpected entry point, which is usually poorly reinforced by the enemy, becomes the general's focused access point into the territory. By doing so, the army has done everything it can to guarantee its initial success. From there, the general has the ability to reorganize his troops and decide on the next course of strategic action.

> *"If you chase two rabbits, you will surely lose both."* ~ *African Proverb*

In maintaining intense focus and taking on one strategic area at a time, we often end up having the opportunity to gain even wider influence later on. Deliberate focus leads to diversification over time. Deliberate diversification in the early stages leads to a lack of focus, creating an overleveraged and under-resourced business, or life.

A wild horse is a beautiful creature, but it is not very useful for practical purposes. Because of its tremendous power, a wild horse can cause an incredible amount of damage. To make a horse useful, a trainer must put it through a process called 'breaking.' In this process, the trainer disciplines the horse until the horse's will aligns with the trainer's will. Once this happens, the sovereign hand of its master directs the strength of the animal.

In the same way, our brokenness leads to healthy submission and dependence on the true Master, God, when we allow it to. The amazing news in all of this is that we have a Master who is 'good' in the truest definition of the word. He leads us on paths of wholeness and righteousness. He takes us on adventures that we could never dream of. He guides us always towards Life, even when it doesn't feel like it, and even when it doesn't look like it.

In submission to the true King, we also learn the boundless power of meekness. Meekness is not weakness. Meekness is power under control.

Here, living *Unleashed*, ironically, is to have your life fully controlled. The difference is that your life is controlled by Freedom Himself. To live completely *Unleashed*, our decisions must be directed by the highest source of Wisdom. Interestingly, when the Spirit of the Creator governs our lives most completely is when we experience the utmost freedom. The more we submit to God, the freer we become to unleash the full potential of our highest selves. Through this healthy submission, we lose our false selves and gain our true identities wrapped up in the Divine. In this way one allows the individual drop of water of his or her life to become one with the endless ocean of Life itself. Here, the finite become infinite.

When setting out to build a wall, do not continue to make the terrible mistake, like many of us naturally do, of throwing a bunch of random, different shapes and sizes of multicolored bricks in an area hoping that they form themselves into something useful. Instead your only task, once you have a solid grasp for the overall vision of what the wall is supposed to look like, is to methodically and deliberately take one brick at a time and place it as perfectly as you can. Once you have finished *carefully* (in the true sense of the word 'carefully,' which is 'with great care') laying the first brick, you then grab the next brick and place it meticulously in its place. Repeat this process over and over, laying each brick with just as much intentionality – taking the time to step back ever so often to examine the big-picture so as to ensure you are on the right track for the overall vision, adjusting the vision as needed – until the wall is finished. It may feel like we're not making much progress, but we can only build a good wall one brick at a time.

Focus is a powerful tool. It is what transforms regular sunlight into an intense, fire-starting, source of heat through the use of a magnifying glass. Passion, directed through the magnifying glass of focus, is what finally turns our dreams into realities. It becomes a controlled fire that provides warmth and life to those around us.

Don't half-ass two things.

Whole-ass one thing.

REFLECTION:

What should I be focusing on right now?

Keep in mind that it may not be something that feels fun to do at the moment. Sometimes we do what we have to do so we can do what we want to do.

CHAPTER 13

How to Fail Better

This book is late. Writing it has taken much more time and energy than it should have. I say that the book is late simply because I noticed the seed in my soul that contained the vision for writing this volume several years ago, and I did not act on it at that time. Something held me back for years. (Of course, on a metaphysical level, this book is right on time. It is neither early nor late. It simply is. And it required all of the learning and life lessons, now poured out on these pages, which came to me all the way up until the moment of its completion. Yet for the purpose of this illustration, we'll consider the book to be late.)

There are a few reasons for the delay, not good ones, but they are reasons. Foremost, I believe that the fear of humiliation has held me back from releasing this work to the world.

I'm not sure I subscribe to the incredible reverence our society gives to the monster we call the 'fear of failure.' In our exploration of 'failure-dreading' as a barrier to momentum, I think we've stopped too early on that path. If I'm honest it is not really failure that I'm afraid of. It's the fear of failing *in front of people* that has left me feeling paralyzed at times, people whose opinions of me carry unhealthy amounts of weight in shaping how I view myself and what paths I choose to take. I know that at times I have delayed or even fully surrendered God-given dreams because others think those undertakings impractical or unnecessary.

Ultimately, we fear the judgments of our failures, not the failures themselves. If we weren't afraid of being ashamed, I think we'd attempt every one of the meaningful dreams that stir passion in our hearts.

What would you attempt if you knew you couldn't fail?

If we understood that 'failure' has no shame attached to it, we'd fail as much as we could, because the experiences alone, along with the valuable lessons we learn because of them, would be worth the ride. Life would be exhilarating regardless of whether or not we've achieved some arbitrary form of success. If you were building a shelter on a deserted island, you wouldn't give any mental or emotional energy towards the useless state-of-being called the 'fear of failure.' You would just build, do your best, hope it's functional, and call it a day. But now let's introduce some other humans to the mix. The moment there are other people around to judge our work, it changes the game. It shouldn't change anything, but it does. All of a sudden we start to care what people might think. We don't necessarily fear failure itself; we fear others' judgments of our failure.

What would you do if you didn't care what other people were going to say? How would it change the way you lived if you weren't consumed by the petty opinions of others, even the people that matter to you? And what dreams would you pursue if you could just stop submitting to the whims of the worst critic of all – your inner critic?

So with this book, I've been afraid of putting it out there. I've had to work diligently to silence the critics, both the real ones and the ones that I created in my own imagination. In my mind, there are all kinds of people saying hurtful things about a book that, at the time, had yet to be written. Not all of the critics came across as ill-intentioned, either. Some just spoke of the impracticality of my undertaking. Others pointed out the simple fact that I didn't do well in high school English class. "And who do you think you are to write a book?" others asked. As mentioned in an earlier chapter, words carry even more power when they come from people who are close to us. Words carry the most power when we have gone as far as to accept these ideas as our own. That applies to positive messages as well as to negative messages.

I'm now positive that children are wiser than adults. A friend of mine likes to lead people in an activity called 'prophetic drawings.' In this activity, he divides people into pairs, and asks them to quiet themselves and listen to their souls to get a message from God for the other person. Then with whatever comes to mind, they are to draw a picture for their activity partner, which represents what they think God is saying. The results are astonishing. Even people who don't think they can hear God can end up getting meaningful messages from the Creator for another person. It's amazing what happens when we slow down and quiet ourselves enough to listen.

I was struck with the simple beauty of this activity. But I was even more touched by the odd trend that my friend noticed in leading this activity numerous times.

When leading the activity for a group of adults, it would consistently go something like this. After people had taken time to be still and listen, they would draw their pictures. Then, after a few minutes of drawing, my friend would tell everyone that it was time to show the other person the picture. With the adults, there was always some giggling and awkward maneuvering as they said things like, "I'm not an artist, so don't judge the picture." The adults would often have to qualify their drawings, and when they finally got the courage to show them to the other person, it was done so abashedly and reservedly.

Leading this activity for a group of young kids produced a much different outcome. When it was time for the kids to show each other their pictures, there was no awkward squirming, no explanations as to why the other person shouldn't take their pictures seriously, or embarrassed giggling at the silliness of their own drawings.

No. Instead, they were just excited to hand their artwork to the other kids. They were proud of their work and they wanted their activity partner to see what they had created. It was as if they intrinsically knew a deeper truth. There was no explanation necessary because they knew at an unconscious level that it was the best they could do. So who cares what anyone else thinks? This is my picture. I drew it. I gave it all I had. Now, the other person can enjoy it.

Simple.

Five-year-olds don't typically make objectively beautiful pieces of art when they draw. But they really don't care. When a five-year-old draws a picture for his or her parents, they finish the image and with joy they hand it to the adult. And we all know what moms or dads are likely to do with these ugly pictures. They put it up on their fridges and celebrate the creations. Kids know this. We should learn from them.

> *"Courage is not the absence of fear, but rather the judgment that something else is more important than fear."*
>
> ~ *Ambrose Redmoon*

It seems to be around the age of 10 years old when this deep understanding of our own inherent worth begins to dissolve for most of us. It is at this age that we really start to pay attention to what other people think of us. We start to pay attention to what other people are going to say about our work, our choices, our style, our appearance. From here, most of us start becoming increasingly self-conscious about putting our true selves out to the world. By the time we become adults, it takes a concerted effort to undo this destructive mindset.

And so it was with this book. I was afraid of putting my work out there. I realized that I had a lot to learn from children; the Kingdom of Heaven belongs to such as these for a good reason. I decided that I would handle this book like a child handles a hand-drawn picture. I would make it, giving it my very best, and I would give it to my Papa (God).

I knew deep down, that if this book were a picture, God would hang it on His fridge. I will live my life like a kid who is excited to show off his creations to his Papa. I will evaluate myself only on whether or not I gave it my all, doing my work with passion and heart. And when I give it to God, He will celebrate my work. It would not necessarily be because the book, or whatever other creation, is incredible from the point of view of other humans; it would just be because He's proud of His son.

I decided to write this book for an audience of One. I'm writing for God. And if others happen to enjoy it, that becomes a humbling bonus. If the book goes nowhere and not even my own mother reads it, it may sting briefly, but it really wouldn't matter because I didn't write it for any human anyway. Living for an audience of One removes all fear, especially when it comes to creating beauty in the world. Here we are able to find the honesty of the soul. We become able to create from a place of authenticity and we are able to live fully, without the fear of humiliation.

If you please God, it doesn't matter whom you displease.

If you displease God, it doesn't matter whom you please.

PRINCIPLE #13: LEARN TO FAIL WELL

At some point, the importance of our missions has to eclipse the opinions of others and our own self-doubts. What would you create if you weren't thinking about what other people would think? Life can discourage the creativity right out of us if we're not careful to protect it.

@goodtripinc

A university professor of mine once recounted a story to our class that has remained with me to this day. He spoke of when he spent a considerable amount of time living with a tribe of First Nations people in northern Canada. In a discussion with the chief, while recounting a story from his past, the professor mentioned that he lamented having made a certain 'big mistake' in his life.

At that point, the chief stopped him and asked, "What do you mean by 'mistake'?"

To which the professor replied, "Well, it means that I messed up and did something that I regret."

"Ah, in our language," the chief continued, "we don't have the word 'mistake.' The closest word that we have to that idea translates more closely to the English word for 'learning.' We don't make mistakes. We only make 'learnings.' It would only be what you call a 'mistake' if we didn't learn."

We learn by trying. But most of us are too paralyzed by all of the things that could go wrong to actually make some attempts. Just as Thomas Edison reportedly discovered thousands upon thousands of ways *not* to make a lightbulb while attempting his invention, we, too, learn many ways *not* to do things while on our journeys towards meaningful breakthroughs. In this regard, failure is a beautiful thing. Failure may actually be the only way forward.

If we're not failing, it means we're not trying. If we're not trying, we're not going anywhere at all. May we learn to fail well. When we give a project our all, we find out much more quickly what works and what doesn't. If we're living *Unleashed*, we should be failing often because we're attempting things outside of our comfort zones. And when we're focused on learning from our missteps, we should be making new mistakes instead of repeating the old ones.

"It is not the critic who counts; not the man who points out how the strong man stumbles, or where the doer of deeds could have done them better. The credit belongs to the man who is actually in the arena, whose face is marred by dust and sweat and blood; who strives valiantly; who errs, who comes short again and again, because there is no effort without error and shortcoming; but who does actually strive to do the deeds; who knows great enthusiasms, the great devotions; who spends himself in a worthy cause; who at the best knows in the end the triumph of high achievement, and who at the worst, if he fails, at least fails while daring greatly, so that his place shall never be with those cold and timid souls who neither know victory nor defeat."

~ Franklin D. Roosevelt

REFLECTION:

How well am I failing right now?

Am I taking good risks?

Or am I just trying to stay comfortable?

CHAPTER 14

How to Get to the Point

This may be disappointing to learn at first, but it should be freeing once we grasp the reality of it. The fact is that ultimately there is no 'destination' to be had, at least not in the way that we humans like to chart our progress and our goals. We like to know when it is that we've finally *arrived*, whatever that means.

The freeing news is that the journey *is* the destination. And the ultimate destination is Love. Love is the only thing worth keeping our sights on. It is the only way to know whether or not we're on the best paths. Love is the only way to know that we've made it. When we measure our lives by the love that we manifest and share with others, we've measured life by Life itself. We enter ultimate reality.

It takes intense heat in order to refine silver into its purest form. In this process, the refiner starts by placing the silver in a pot, over a small fire. As the silver heats up, the impurities rise to the surface and the refiner scrapes them out and discards them. When this is done, the refiner adds more heat to the fire. With increased heat, new impurities rise to the surface and are removed once more. The refiner increases the heat slowly, repeating this process until he has fully refined silver at his disposal. The refiner knows that he has completed his work when he can see his perfect reflection in the silver.

God takes us through this refining process. He turns up the heat of our lives, bit by bit, never using more heat than is necessary, removing impurities each time until He can see His nature reflected in us. The purpose of life is to become more and more like Him. We were made in His image. The journey of life serves to return us to this image, to our truest selves.

PRINCIPLE #14: STAY IN THE FIRE

Whatever path you choose to embark on, know that the path will shape you along the way. God is far less concerned with what we accomplish in this lifetime and far more concerned with who we become in the process.

There will be joy. There will be pain. There will be fulfillment. There will be emptiness. All of this is normal. The result of the process is worth all of the pain of the path.

Along the journey, we find ourselves further equipped with resources. We find ourselves growing in our capacities to achieve and to love more deeply because of the lessons we've learned. Know that a bumpy road isn't necessarily a bad thing. Being out of your comfort zone, when heading in a healthy direction, is where growth happens.

> *"Smooth seas never made a skilled sailor."* ~ *African Proverb*

Love isn't easy, but love is the reason we exist. If we have love for ourselves, for others, and for God, we have everything. When we love, we are tapping into God, who is Love itself. Love is the whole point. And it's what moves us towards beautiful action.

Finally, it would be silly to talk about living *Unleashed* without mentioning the source of power needed to do this. We need God's power to accomplish anything worthwhile, whether we acknowledge Him as the source or not. Trying to live *Unleashed* without tapping into the ultimate source of energy would be like trying to drive a broken-down, empty car with flat tires, without fixing it up and putting fuel in it. At best, you can try to push the car around. Or you may get lucky and roll the car down a hill for a short period of time. But you're not going very far or very fast trying to live like this.

> *"When you seek Me you will find Me when you search with all of your heart."* ~ *God*

This is why so many of us feel like we're exerting a ton of effort and not getting anywhere. It's because we're still trying to push our broken lives around using our own strength and we have yet to fill up with the right fuel or get the Great Mechanic's help to heal our brokenness. The Spirit of the Creator is the power-source we're missing. If you'd like to experience this source of power, ask God for it and seek out the path of Life for yourself. I dare you.

Now go. The life-force inside of you must not be wasted. The world needs what you have.

It is time for you to live *Unleashed*.

"A rough and unshapen log has no idea that it can be made into a statue that will be considered a masterpiece, but the carver sees what can be done with it. So many... do not understand that God can mold them into saints, until they put themselves into the hands of that almighty Artisan."

~ St. Ignatius of Loyola

REFLECTION:

On this journey, who am I becoming?

"Forward: The Direction Bravery is Required"

Artist: Matthew Douglas 2018

This piece is part of an art exhibit focused on combating human trafficking by creating awareness and raising proceeds through the sale of the artwork.

How to Go Through Hell

Here is what I've observed as the nature of the narrow path. If you ever embark on a creative journey, whether starting a business, creating a piece of art, launching into a new career, or taking a path towards any kind of healthy growth, then you are likely to experience the following. These are what I believe are the six inevitable steps in the process of creating beauty in the world:

Step 1: This is awesome!

In this exciting step, you love your idea and believe that you are the champion of the world. All you see is opportunity and the positives of how the world will be a better place when you succeed. As Adidas says, "Impossible is nothing!"

Step 2: This is challenging!

At this point you've already made some concrete plans, stopped talking about it, and you're at least more than a month into the journey of actually doing real stuff. You now notice the presence of what you consider to be *interesting* new obstacles that you didn't foresee. You still press on, buzzing, though a bit less intensely, from the initial beauty and magnetism of your new idea. At this point, you may be tempted towards distractions, anything that will take you away from doing the hard work of moving forward.

Step 3: This is horrible!

Here, everything seems to be going wrong and you have to fight hard just to remember why you started this process at all. Getting out of bed to work on your project isn't exhilarating anymore. When you go to family functions, the people who care about you tell you to "get a real job and to stop trying to accomplish more than you should." Your mind yells at you at every opportunity it has, saying, "Worst. Idea. Ever."

Step 4: I'M horrible!

At this point you've gotten past focusing on the glaring obstacles on your path and you start to believe that you've found the real problem: YOU. At this point, you may start believing that you are actually just a terrible human being, and that's why things aren't working. Possibly even the worst one that has ever lived. You wonder if your uncle was right about you needing a real job.

Step 5: This could actually turn out to be awesome!

You have officially crawled out of the pit of self-loathing enough to realize that you're not completely broken. You know you have shortcomings, but you now realize those are natural and that you need some help to get to where you're trying to go. You realize that you are part of the problem, but the solution is to keep going and grow in your capacity, not to shrink back and stop now. You see some new challenges, but you're cautiously beginning to feel some excited energy in your soul for the first time in a while because you realize that there is a light at the end of the dark tunnel.

Step 6: This is SO awesome!!!

Congratulations! You've persevered to the point where you realize that ups and downs are normal and you're so happy that you stuck with the plan. You're tapping into the beauty of being who you were created to be and making the world a better place as a result. Making a lasting difference is a natural outflow of 'being' and it feels SO good. You couldn't see yourself trying to play 'small', trying to 'fit-in', or living a boring life ever again!

This is a greatly oversimplified version of the journey and this process is cyclical in nature, meaning that you may repeat some of the steps throughout the journey.

If you find yourself somewhere in the painful middle of this journey, don't stop. Feel the feels. Grow forward. You will make it. It will be OK.

"This, too, shall pass." ~ *Ancient Proverb*

If you're going through hell, keep going. Remember, you didn't come this far to only come this far.

Acknowledgements

God, you're the source of life. My darling Natalie, you love me so well on our journey together. My beautiful children, even thinking of you is enough inspiration to carry me through the hardest days. My loving parents, I can see further because I stand on your strong shoulders. My incredible community, you continue to support me deeply. My longsuffering friends, for some reason you've never given up on me. Trevor, I can't thank you enough for believing in me and in this venture. Amanda, thank you for your painstaking edits to make this legible. Thank you to all of the *Unleashed* humans living fully and doing things that matter who shared their wisdom for this project.

Finally, a huge thank you to my Kickstarter supporters:

Craig R., Felisha, Mike, Bronwyn, Erika, Connor, Teesha, Lana, Jolene, Helen, Shayne, Craig S., Josh, Clint, Halle, Russ, Noreen, Michelle, Laura-Megan, Sabrina, Sam, Andrew, Joel, Solomon, Brian, Sean, Dana, Billy, Ruthie, Jennifer, Shahir, Katie, Hannah, Larry, Louise, Devon, Vicki, Sandra, Tri, Danny, Nicole, Sarah, Rachel, Heather, Wanda, Nancy, Taylor, Dan, Samson, Nick, Kyle, Kayla, Jim, Polly, Kaleb, Elena, and Lon.

Your backing is what made this vision real.

Connect

Justin loves people. So if you're a person, he would love to hear from you. Email him at hello@justinminott.com

For information on having Justin inspire your audience by speaking at your event, please visit justinminott.com/speaking.

Made in the USA
Lexington, KY
03 November 2019